P9-DLZ-559

Fracking

Other Books in the Current Controversies Series

Drones
Genetic Engineering
Homelessness and Street Crime
LGBTQ Rights
Political Correctness
Privacy and Security in the Digital Age
Returning Soldiers and PTSD
The Border Wall with Mexico
The Political Elite and Special Interests

Fracking

Anne Cunningham, Book Editor

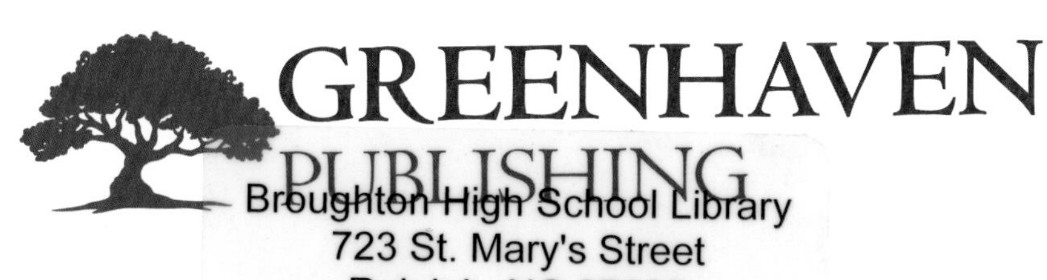

Published in 2018 by Greenhaven Publishing, LLC
353 3rd Avenue, Suite 255, New York, NY 10010

First Edition

Articles in Greenhaven Publishing anthologies are often edited for length to meet page requirements. In addition, original titles of these works are changed to clearly present the main thesis and to explicitly indicate the author's opinion. Every effort is made to ensure that Greenhaven Publishing accurately reflects the original intent of the authors. Every effort has been made to trace the owners of the copyrighted material.

Cover image: Zoonar GmbH/Alamy Stock Photo

Library of Congress Cataloging-in-Publication Data

Names: Cunningham, Anne C., editor.
Title: Fracking / edited by Anne C. Cunningham.
Other titles: Fracking (New York, N.Y.)
Description: First edition. | New York : Greenhaven Publishing, 2018. | Series: Current controversies | Includes bibliographical references and index. | Audience: Grades 9-12.
Identifiers: LCCN 2017008136| ISBN 9781534501034 (library bound) | ISBN 9781534501010 (pbk.)
Subjects: LCSH: Gas wells--Environmental aspects. | Hydraulic fracturing--Environmental aspects.
Classification: LCC TD195.G3 F695 2018 | DDC 622/.3381--dc23
LC record available at https://lccn.loc.gov/2017008136

Manufactured in the United States of America

Website: http://greenhavenpublishing.com

Contents

Foreword 11

Introduction 14

Chapter 1: Will Fracking Eliminate Our Dependency on Coal?

Overview: The Costs and Benefits of Fracking 18

John Wihbey

Natural gas burns cleaner than coal, and is therefore touted by proponents as a "bridge fuel" suited to address climate change. But fracking has many downsides as well. These include water pollution, earthquakes, and disincentives toward renewable energy.

Yes: Fracking Is a Viable Substitute for Coal

Fracking Is an Important Part of Our Energy Future 25

Max Luke, Ted Nordhaus, Michael Shellenberger, and Alex Trembath

Innovative energy production is essential for America. Fracking is one such innovation. We now have a vast supply of natural gas, at a low per-million BTU price. EPA plans to phase out coal-fired power plants in favor of gas provide benefits for the environment and customers.

Fracking Is Helpful in the Short Term 33

Alison Singer

If regulated properly, fracking can help America meet its energy needs. Over the long term, cleaner renewable technologies are needed to wean us off fossil fuel dependence and prevent catastrophic climate effects.

Coal Seam Gas Can Provide Australia With Clean Energy 37

Dennis Cooke

Australia relies on brown coal for energy. Since coal seam gas provides equivalent energy with half the carbon emissions, it would be beneficial for Australia to use this fuel. Concerns about pollution and flammable water could stand in the way.

There are many opportunities for "fugitive" methane gas to leak from fracking operations. Energy companies and regulators are working to address these technical issues, aiming to keep methane leakage below the 1 percent level deemed safe.

Study Shows Methane Emission from Fracking Is Low 89

Steve Everley

A joint study by University of Texas and the Environmental Defense Fund showed a marked decrease in methane emissions from fracking sites. The report suggests that the technology employed by the industry to detect and repair methane leaks is working.

Sierra Club Credits Natural Gas for Reducing Carbon Emissions 94

Seth Whitehead

Leading environmental organizations such as the Sierra Club are recognizing the role of natural gas in reducing carbon emissions. The Sierra Club still advocates moving "beyond natural gas", as other negatives of fracking such as water pollution potentially offset such gains.

No: Fracking-Related Methane Leaks Could Push Climate Change over the "Tipping Point"

People Near Fracking Sites See Increased Risk of Health Problems 98

National Resource Defense Council

A comprehensive analysis by the National Resource Defense Council (NRDC) cites numerous health risks including respiratory problems and increased risks of cancer impacting workers and others in close proximity to gas wells.

Fracking Pollutes the Air 102

Jesse Coleman

Methane leaks from fracking wells cause major greenhouse pollutants. For this reason, Colorado governor John Hickenlooper has proposed regulations to address these potential harms as fracking gains momentum across the state.

Fracking Will Not Reduce Net Greenhouse Gas Emission 105

Alex Kirby

Market forces will offset net environmental gains of replacing coal with relatively cleaner burning natural gas. According to computer simulations, a high supply will keep gas prices low. This will likely nullify any small advantage fracking promises for the atmospheric reduction of greenhouse gas.

Chapter 3: Does Fracking Endanger Our Water Supply?

Overview: There Is Conflict About Fracking's Impact on the Water Supply **109**

Greenpeace
Fracking is a highly water-intensive activity. In addition to unearthing saline and possibly radioactive water, wastewater and migrating gas from fracking may contaminate drinking water supplies.

Yes: Fracking Is Very Dangerous to Drinking Water Supplies

Fracking Waste Contaminates Groundwater **117**

Gayathri Vaidyanathan
A peer-reviewed study of the Wind River Basin of Wyoming by former EPA scientist Dominic DiGiulio has shown that waste from hydraulic fracturing contaminates water supplies. Encana Corp. countered with tests showing the water is safe.

EPA Study Identifies Risk of Water Contamination from Fracking **124**

Elizabeth Shogren
A new study published by the EPA claims fracking is unlikely to cause "widespread" water contamination. This does not mean fracking is safe. The report identifies several risks it poses to water, and concludes that more research is necessary to determine the long-term impacts of fracking on water supplies.

Controversy Surrounds Wyoming Study of Water Contamination **128**

Scott Tong
Residents of the small town of Pavillion, Wyoming, suspected that fracking was poisoning their water. An EPA report stated contamination was likely, but then handed the study over to the state of Wyoming, who argued that widespread contamination was unlikely. Now, authors of a new academic study are provoking further controversy by upholding the EPA's original suspicions.

No: Earthquakes Are Complex Natural Phenomena

There Is Little Scientific Evidence Linking Fracking to Earthquakes **162**

Marita Noon

The media was quick to blame fracking for Oklahoma's recent earthquake, its most powerful on record. Here, Marita Noon suggests that wastewater produced by conventional oil and gas drilling, not fracking, was more likely responsible for the increased seismic activity.

Experts Say Fracking Not the Cause of Oklahoma Earthquakes **167**

Seth Whitehead

Seth Whitehead argues that wastewater disposal caused the recent powerful earthquake in Oklahoma. While some in the media have blamed fracking, Whitehead cites the expert opinion that longstanding practices in conventional extraction are more likely to blame.

Organizations to Contact **174**

Bibliography **178**

Index **181**

Foreword

"Controversy" is a word that has an undeniably unpleasant connotation. It carries a definite negative charge. Controversy can spoil family gatherings, spread a chill around classroom and campus discussion, inflame public discourse, open raw civic wounds, and lead to the ouster of public officials. We often feel that controversy is almost akin to bad manners, a rude and shocking eruption of that which must not be spoken or thought of in polite, tightly guarded society. To avoid controversy, to quell controversy, is often seen as a public good, a victory for etiquette, perhaps even a moral or ethical imperative.

Yet the studious, deliberate avoidance of controversy is also a whitewashing, a denial, a death threat to democracy. It is a false sterilizing and sanitizing and superficial ordering of the messy, ragged, chaotic, at times ugly processes by which a healthy democracy identifies and confronts challenges, engages in passionate debate about appropriate approaches and solutions, and arrives at something like a consensus and a broadly accepted and supported way forward. Controversy is the megaphone, the speaker's corner, the public square through which the citizenry finds and uses its voice. Controversy is the life's blood of our democracy and absolutely essential to the vibrant health of our society.

Our present age is certainly no stranger to controversy. We are consumed by fierce debates about technology, privacy, political correctness, poverty, violence, crime and policing, guns, immigration, civil and human rights, terrorism, militarism, environmental protection, and gender and racial equality. Loudly competing voices are raised every day, shouting opposing opinions, putting forth competing agendas, and summoning starkly different visions of a utopian or dystopian future. Often these voices attempt to shout the others down; there is precious little listening and considering among the cacophonous din. Yet listening and considering, too, are essential to the health of a democracy. If controversy is democracy's lusty lifeblood, respectful listening and careful thought are its higher faculties, its brain, its conscience.

Current Controversies does not shy away from or attempt to hush the loudly competing voices. It seeks to provide readers with as wide and representative as possible a range of articulate voices on any given controversy of the day, separates each one out to allow it to be heard clearly and fairly, and encourages careful listening to each of these well-crafted, thoughtfully expressed opinions, supplied by some of today's leading academics, thinkers, analysts, politicians, policy makers, economists, activists, change agents, and advocates. Only after listening to a wide range of opinions on an issue, evaluating the strengths and weaknesses of each argument, assessing how well the facts and available evidence mesh with the stated opinions and conclusions, and thoughtfully and critically examining one's own beliefs and conscience can the reader begin to arrive at his or her own conclusions and articulate his or her own stance on the spotlighted controversy.

This process is facilitated and supported in each Current Controversies volume with an introduction and chapter overviews that provide readers with the essential context they need to begin engaging with the spotlighted controversies, with the debates surrounding them, and with their own perhaps shifting or nascent opinions on them. Chapters are organized around several key questions that are answered with diverse opinions representing all points on the political spectrum. In its content, organization, and methodology, readers are encouraged to determine the authors' point of view and purpose, interrogate and analyze the various arguments and their rhetoric and structure, evaluate the arguments' strengths and weaknesses, test their claims against available facts and evidence, judge the validity of the reasoning, and bring into clearer, sharper focus the reader's own beliefs and conclusions and how they may differ from or align with those in the collection or those of classmates.

Research has shown that reading comprehension skills improve dramatically when students are provided with compelling, intriguing, and relevant "discussable" texts. The subject matter of these collections could not be more compelling, intriguing, or urgently relevant to today's students and the world they are poised to inherit. The anthologized articles also provide the basis for stimulating, lively, and passionate classroom debates. Students who are compelled to anticipate objections to their own argument and identify the flaws in those of an opponent read more carefully, think more critically, and steep themselves in relevant context, facts, and information more thoroughly. In short, using discussable text of the kind provided by every single volume in the Current Controversies series encourages close reading, facilitates reading comprehension, fosters research, strengthens critical thinking, and greatly enlivens and energizes classroom discussion and participation. The entire learning process is deepened, extended, and strengthened.

If we are to foster a knowledgeable, responsible, active, and engaged citizenry, we must provide readers with the intellectual, interpretive, and critical-thinking tools and experience necessary to make sense of the world around them and of the all-important debates and arguments that inform it. We must encourage them not to run away from or attempt to quell controversy but to embrace it in a responsible, conscientious, and thoughtful way, to sharpen and strengthen their own informed opinions by listening to and critically analyzing those of others. This series encourages respectful engagement with and analysis of current controversies and competing opinions and fosters a resulting increase in the strength and rigor of one's own opinions and stances. As such, it helps readers assume their rightful place in the public square and provides them with the skills necessary to uphold their awesome responsibility—guaranteeing the continued and future health of a vital, vibrant, and free democracy.

Introduction

Hydraulic fracturing, more commonly known as "fracking", is a method of extracting natural gas and petroleum resources from rock formations deep within the earth. To recover these valuable fossil fuels, highly pressurized liquid is injected horizontally into shale rock. This fracking fluid consists of millions of gallons of water, "proppants" such as sand or metal particles, and secret, proprietary blends of chemicals, many of which are suspected to be toxic. Once injected, the fluid creates cracks and fissures through which gas trapped in rock can flow out. The gas is collected in surface wells, while the tremendous amount of wastewater that results is pumped deep underground for disposal.

Though fracking was developed in the 1950s, the technique has become widespread in the past few decades. This is primarily due to the depletion of oil and gas reserves easily recoverable through conventional means. Fossil fuel companies have invested heavily in fracking in gas rich regions of the United States such as the Marcellus Shale of Pennsylvania and the Barnett Shale in Texas. These companies are seeing huge profits as a result. Nearby residents are worried that the risks of fracking are not understood sufficiently. Environmentalists and ordinary citizens alike are concerned that the fossil fuel industry's vast public relations budget is being mobilized to downplay the many dangers fracking poses to humans and the environment.

Indeed, fracking has become nearly synonymous with this controversy. Despite the considerable economic benefits of fracking, the practice must be weighed as a whole against mounting evidence of the serious health and environmental risks, and other quality of life tradeoffs that follow in its wake. These risks include water contamination, air pollution, and earthquakes. Communities where fracking occurs are often disturbed by the sudden influx of oil and gas infrastructure, and heavy vehicle traffic clogging roadways. For areas such as the Barnett Shale where water is scarce, the diversion of water supplies is taxing and ill advised. For these reasons, many states including Maryland, New Jersey, and Ohio have placed moratoriums on fracking. In Europe, the practice has been banned outright in several countries such as Germany, France, and Scotland.

The viewpoints in this resource examine the fracking debate from both pro and anti stances. They will be of great use to readers seeking balanced information on fracking, and the larger issues of energy policy and environmental protection with which it overlaps.

Proponents of fracking point to the large role increased natural gas production has played in moving the US energy economy towards greater independence, as well as fracking's beneficial effects on the economy overall. Increased GDP, lower energy prices, and the creation of many well-paying jobs can all be traced to fracking. More importantly, advocates of fracking cite natural gas as a necessary "bridge fuel" towards clean energy in the absence of reliable utility-scale renewable energy.

Defenders of fracking acknowledge the scientific consensus that climate change is real and that human activity is driving it. According to *Yale Climate Connections,* natural gas emits 40 percent less carbon per unit than coal. Gas-fired electricity plants emit 66 percent less carbon dioxide than older coal plants, and are also more efficient. Thus, replacing older coal-fired power plants with cleaner and more efficient facilities powered by natural gas appears to be a victory for both the economy and the environment.

Unfortunately, once the disadvantages of fracking are taken into account, the reality is more ambiguous. A 2010 documentary film called *Gasland* depicted flammable water flowing from a tap, indicating its contamination from a nearby fracking operation. The image soon became iconic, galvanizing a large anti-fracking movement, with celebrities such as Mark Ruffalo taking up the cause. Still, defenders of fracking insisted it was safe. Who is right?

Complicating this answer is the fact that non-biased, peer reviewed scientific studies of fracking's impacts on the environment have been very slow to surface. One example is the problem of water contamination in Pavillion, Wyoming. Almost a decade ago, residents of this area noticed a peculiar odor and color to their water. This instigated an EPA study of fracking's possible link to water pollution. Midway through the process the study was turned over the state, which failed to complete it. Some suggest the EPA deliberately failed to publish information alerting the public to dangers of fracking. This may be due to fossil fuel industry lobbying power, and because negative results would contradict the Obama administration's "all of the above" energy policy, which explicitly endorsed fracking. Indeed, just weeks before President Obama left office, the EPA finally released their long delayed report titled *Hydraulic Fracturing for Oil and Gas: Impacts from the Hydraulic Fracturing Water Cycle on Drinking Water Resources in the United States.* The report outlines six likely ways fracking harms water resources.

Even in the face of this evidence, many are unwilling to abandon fracking due to its economic benefits. Oil and gas companies insist that technical advances will reduce accidents and leaks, making fracking safe for all. For those who live near fracking sites, clean drinking water cannot be viewed as just another tradeoff–it is a vital life necessity. The controversy over fracking highlights many of these major problems with our energy economy. Solutions will require knowledge and engagement. The viewpoints in *Current Controversies: Fracking* will help readers reach informed positions on the contentious fracking debate, and may engender activism as well.

CHAPTER 1

Will Fracking Eliminate Our Dependency on Coal?

Overview: The Costs and Benefits of Fracking

John Wihbey

John Wihbey is an assistant professor of journalism and new media at Northeastern University, where he teaches in the Media Innovation program and is a faculty member with the NULab for Texts, Maps, and Networks.

There's an issue where the underlying science remains a political football, and scientists are regularly challenged and called out personally. Where energy needs and short-term economic growth are set against our children's health and future. Where the consequences of bad, short-sighted decisions may be borne primarily by a small subset of under-served and undeserving persons. And where the very descriptive terms in the debate are radioactive, words spun as epithets.

We're not talking here about global warming, and "deniers" versus "warmists." We're talking about the game-changing new set of unconventional oil and gas extraction technologies and techniques collectively known as hydraulic fracturing, or "fracking."

Ask the most hardcore of pro-fracking boosters for their take, and they'll describe the modern miracle of America's new-found energy independence, a reality almost inconceivable just a decade ago. For them, the oil and gas boom around the U.S. has helped to reboot the economy at a time of great need. Prices at the pump have plummeted. Sure, they may acknowledge, there are a few safety issues to be worked out and techniques yet to be perfected, but just look at the big picture.

Fracking detractors in environmental and social justice circles, meanwhile, will conjure up the iconic image: Flammable water flowing from a home faucet. And with that come other haunting images: The double-crossed landowner hapless in the face of

"Pros and Cons of Fracking: 5 Key Issues," by John Wihbey, Yale Climate Connections, May 27, 2015. http://www.yaleclimateconnections.org/2015/05/pros-and-cons-of-fracking-5-key-issues/.

aggressive Big Energy. The ugly rigs rising up amid the tranquility of America's farm, pasture, and suburban lands. The stench of unknown—even secret—chemicals, sickness, and looming illnesses, and death.

Refereeing these confrontations is no easy thing, and unlike the "settled science" of climate change and its causes, the science of fracking is far from settled. But a review of the research can help clarify some of the chief points of contention.

If there's a single source plausibly seen as the fairest, most comprehensive, and cogent assessment, it might be the 2014 literature review published in Annual Reviews of Environment and Resources. It's titled "The Environmental Costs and Benefits of Fracking," authored by researchers affiliated with leading universities and research organizations who reviewed more than 160 studies.

Below are the arguments and synthesized evidence on some key issues, based on the available research literature and conversations with diverse experts.

Air Quality, Health, and the Energy Menu

ISSUE: The new supply of natural gas reachable by fracking is now changing the overall picture for U.S. electricity generation, with consequences for air quality.

PRO FRACKING: Increasing reliance on natural gas, rather than coal, is indisputably creating widespread public health benefits, as the burning of natural gas produces fewer harmful particles in the air. The major new supply of natural gas produced through fracking is displacing the burning of coal, which each year contributes to the early death of thousands of people. Coal made up about 50 percent of U.S. electricity generation in 2008, 37 percent by 2012; meanwhile, natural gas went from about 20 percent to about 30 percent during that same period. In particular, nitrogen oxide and sulfur dioxide emissions have been reduced dramatically. Fracking saves lives, and it saves them right now and not at some indiscernible date well into the future.

CON FRACKING: First, it is not the case that a new natural gas facility coming online always replaces a legacy coal-fired power plant. It may displace coal in West Virginia or North Carolina, but less so in Texas and across the West. So fracking is no sure bet for improving regional air quality. Second, air quality dynamics around fracking operations are not fully understood, and cumulative health impacts of fracking for nearby residents and workers remain largely unknown. Some of the available research evidence from places such as Utah and Colorado suggests there may be under-appreciated problems with air quality, particularly relating to ozone. Further, natural gas is not a purely clean and renewable source of energy, and so its benefits are only relative. It is not the answer to truly cleaning up our air, and in fact could give pause to a much-needed and well thought-out transition to wind, solar, geothermal, and other sources that produce fewer or no harmful airborne fine particulates.

Greenhouse Gas Leaks, Methane and Fugitive Emissions

ISSUE: The extraction process results in some greenhouse gas emissions leakage.

PRO FRACKING: We know that, at the power plant level, natural gas produces only somewhere between 44 and 50 percent of the greenhouse gas emissions compared with burning of coal. This is known for certain; it's basic chemistry. That is a gigantic benefit. Further, some research that claims methane is so harmful uses a 20-year time horizon; but over a 100-year time horizon—the way we generally measure global warming potential—methane is not nearly so harmful as claimed. Thus, methane's impact is potent but relatively brief compared with impacts of increased carbon dioxide emissions. The number-one priority must be to reduce the reliance on coal, the biggest threat to the atmosphere right now. Fears about emissions leaks are overblown. Even if the true leakage rate were slightly more than EPA and some states estimate, it is not that dramatic. We are developing technology to reduce these leaks and further narrow the gap. Moreover, research-based modeling suggests that even if energy consumption increases overall, the United States still will reap greenhouse benefits as a result of fracking.

CON FRACKING: Research from Cornell has suggested that leaked methane—a powerful greenhouse gas—from wells essentially wipes out any greenhouse gas benefits of natural gas derived from fracking. And at other points in the life cycle, namely transmission and distribution, there are further ample leaks. Falling natural gas prices will only encourage more energy use, negating any "cleaner" benefits of gas. Finally, there is no question that the embrace of cheap natural gas will undercut incentives to invest in solar, wind, and other renewables. We are at a crucial juncture over the next few decades in terms of reducing the risk of "tipping points" and catastrophic melting of the glaciers. Natural gas is often seen as a "bridge," but it is likely a bridge too far, beyond the point where scientists believe we can go in terms of greenhouse gas levels in the atmosphere.

Drinking Water Wars

ISSUE: Fracking may threaten human health by contaminating drinking water supplies.

PRO FRACKING: It is highly unlikely that well-run drilling operations, which involve extracting oil and gas from thousands of feet down in the ground, are creating cracks that allow chemicals to reach relatively shallow aquifers and surface water supplies. Drinking water and oil and gas deposits are at very different levels in the ground. To the extent that there are problems, we must make sure companies pay more attention to the surface operations and the top 500 to 1,000 feet of piping. But that's not the fracking—that's just a matter of making sure that the steel tubing, the casing, is not leaking and that the cement around it doesn't have cracks. Certain geologies, such as those in Pennsylvania's Marcellus Shale region, do require more care; but research has found that between 2008 and 2011, only a handful of major incidents happened across more than

3,500 wells in the Marcellus. We are learning and getting better. So this is a technical, well-integrity issue, not a deal-breaker. As for the flammable water, it is a fact that flammable water was a reality 100 years ago in some of these areas. It can be made slightly worse in a minority of cases, but it's unlikely and it is often the result of leaks from activities other than fracking. In terms of disclosure, many of the chemicals are listed on data sheets available to first-responders: The information is disclosed to relevant authorities.

CON FRACKING: This April, yet another major study, published in the Proceedings of the National Academy of Sciences, confirmed that high-volume hydraulic fracturing techniques can contaminate drinking water. There have been numerous reports by citizens across the country of fouled tap water; it is a fact that some of the tap water has even turned bubbly and flammable, as a result of increased methane. Well blowouts have happened, and they are a complete hazard to the environment. The companies involved cannot be trusted, and roughly one in five chemicals involved in the fracking process are still classified as trade secrets. Even well-meaning disclosure efforts such as FracFocus.org do not provide sufficient information. And we know that there are many who cut corners out in the field, no matter the federal or state regulations we try to impose. They already receive dozens of violation notices at sites, with little effect. We've created a Gold Rush/Wild West situation by green-lighting all of this drilling, and in the face of these economic incentives, enforcement has little impact.

Infrastructure, Resources, and Communities

ISSUE: Fracking operations are sometimes taking place near and around populated areas, with consequences for the local built and natural environments.

PRO FRACKING: Water intensity is lower for fracking than other fossil fuels and nuclear: Coal, nuclear and oil extraction use approximately two, three, and 10 times, respectively, as much water as fracking per energy unit, and corn ethanol may use

1,000 times more if the plants are irrigated. For communities, the optics, aesthetics, and quality of life issues are real, but it's worth remembering that drilling operations and rigs don't go on forever—it's not like putting up a permanent heavy manufacturing facility. The operations are targeted and finite, and the productivity of wells is steadily rising, getting more value during operations. Moreover, the overall societal benefits outweigh the downsides, which are largely subjective in this respect.

CON FRACKING: More than 15 million Americans have had a fracking operation within a mile of their home. Still, that means that a small proportion of people shoulder the burden and downsides, with no real compensation for this intrusive new industrial presence. Fracking is hugely water-intensive: A well can require anywhere from two- to 20-million gallons of water, with another 25 percent used for operations such as drilling and extraction. It can impact local water sources. The big, heavy trucks beat up our roads over hundreds of trips back-and-forth—with well-documented consequences for local budgets and infrastructure. In places such as Pennsylvania, Ohio, and Colorado, the drilling rigs have popped up near where people have their homes, diminishing the quality of life and creating an industrial feel to some of our communities. This is poor planning at best, and sheer greed at its worst. It seldom involves the preferences of the local residents.

Finally, it's also the case that relatively low impact fees are being charged and relatively little funding is being set aside to mitigate future problems as wells age and further clean-up is necessary. It is the opposite of a sustainable solution, as well production tends to drop sharply after initial fracking. Within just five years, wells may produce just 10 percent of what they did in the first month of operation. In short order, we're likely to have tens of thousands of sealed and abandoned wells all over the U.S. landscape, many of which will need to be monitored, reinforced, and maintained. It is a giant unfunded scheme.

Earthquakes: Seismic Worries

ISSUE: Fracking wells, drilled thousands of feet down, may change geology in a potentially negative way, leading to earthquakes.

PRO FRACKING: Earthquakes are a naturally occurring phenomenon, and even in the few instances where fracking operations likely contributed to them, they were minor. We've had tens of thousands of wells drilled over many years now, and there are practically zero incidents in which operations-induced seismic effects impacted citizens. There's also research to suggest that the potential for earthquakes can be mitigated through safeguards.

CON FRACKING: We are only just beginning to understand what we are doing to our local geologies, and this is dangerous. The 2014 Annual Reviews of Environment and Resources paper notes that "between 1967 and 2000, geologists observed a steady background rate of 21 earthquakes of 3.0 Mw or greater in the central United States per year. Starting in 2001, when shale gas and other unconventional energy sources began to grow, the rate rose steadily to [approximately] 100 such earthquakes annually, with 188 in 2011 alone." New research on seismology in places such as Texas and Oklahoma suggests risky and unknown changes. It is just not smart policy to go headlong first—at massive scale—and only later discover the consequences.

Fracking Is an Important Part of Our Energy Future

Max Luke, Ted Nordhaus, Michael Shellenberger, Alex Trembath

The authors work at Breakthrough Institute. Max Luke is policy expert, Ted Nordhaus is director of research, Alex Trembath is communication director, and Michael Shellenberger is co-founder.

Amid a flurry of regulations and political activism against coal plants, one phenomenon has proved the most effective in killing coal in the United States: the arrival of cheaper, cleaner energy. Natural gas fuels the clean energy revolution by displacing dirtier coal, lowering carbon emissions, providing a platform for deployment of lower-carbon energy technologies, and creating economic surpluses that can be directed towards energy innovation. And while questions have arisen in the last several years regarding the local and global environmental impacts of the shale revolution, a survey of the empirical literature reveals gas to be a highly favorable environmental alternative to coal.

In a new Breakthrough Institute report, Coal Killer: How Natural Gas Fuels the Clean Energy Revolution, we document the energy and environmental benefits of natural gas and gas's exceptional position in accelerating the transition to a zero-carbon future.

The rapid displacement of coal in recent years has allowed the United States to achieve the largest recent carbon emissions reductions of any country in the world. While natural gas poses significant environmental challenges, its benefits over coal are undeniable. Mercury pollution, sulfur oxides and nitrogen oxides, water intensity, and pollution-related costs and mortality are all reliably lower with natural gas than with coal. Methane

"Coal Killer: How Natural Gas Fuels the Clean Energy Revolution," by Ted Nordhaus, Alex Trembath, Michael Shellenberger, and Max Luke, The Breakthrough Institute, June 25, 2013. Reprinted by permission.

leakage mitigation opportunities will typically prove profitable for drillers, and leakage's effects on global climate change will prove relatively minor as long as policymakers sustain efforts to accelerate decarbonization.

While the prospects for zero-carbon technologies like renewables and nuclear are certainly affected by cheap natural gas, worries that the shale revolution will kill zero-carbon energy are overblown. Cheap, flexible natural gas generation will become more and more essential as variable renewable technologies like wind and solar achieve wider penetrations in electricity grids. And while natural gas has been partially responsible for some recent closures of nuclear power plants in the United States, the major challenges faced by nuclear power—high capital and refurbishment costs, regulatory uncertainty, and public skepticism—predate and overwhelm the competitive pressure posed by the American shale revolution. Zero-carbon technologies remain far more dependent on innovation policies than the relative price of natural gas.

The arrival of a cheaper energy technology to displace coal has provided more than $100 billion a year in economic benefits to the United States, and tens of millions in state and federal revenues. Within the next few years the shale revolution will have contributed more to the US economy than all cumulative federal expenditures on all energy industries since 1950. In light of the significant and multi-decade public-private investments that made the shale revolution possible in the first place, some portion of these benefits should be directed towards energy innovation policies and investments.

Energy transitions are not step-wise, perfectly sequential, or spontaneous. From whale oil, wood, and kerosene to coal, petroleum, and natural gas to renewables and nuclear, the evolutionary process from higher-carbon to lower-carbon energy has been accelerated by government policy. The American shale gas revolution offers vital lessons not just for the promise of public investments in energy innovation, but for the nature of decarbonization and how best to target energy and climate policies.

Executive Summary

The rapid replacement of coal by cheaper and cleaner natural gas has helped drive emissions down in the United States more than in any other country in the world in recent years. Cheap natural gas is crushing domestic demand for coal and is the main reason for the rapid decline in US carbon emissions. The gas revolution offers a way for the United States and other nations to replace coal burning while accelerating the transition to zero-carbon energy.

In the United States, coal-powered electricity went from 50 to 37 percent of the generation mix between 2007 and 2012, with the bulk of it replaced by natural gas. Energy transitions typically take many decades to occur, and the evidence suggests that the natural gas revolution is still in its infancy. The successful combination of new drilling, hydraulic fracturing ("fracking"), and underground mapping technologies to cheaply extract gas from shale and other unconventional rock formations has the potential to be as disruptive as past energy technology revolutions—and as beneficial to humans and our natural environment.

This report reviews the evidence and finds that natural gas is a net environmental benefit at local, regional, national, and global levels. In recent years, the rapid expansion of natural gas production has provoked legitimate local concerns about noise, air, water, and methane pollution that should and can be addressed. But the evidence is strong that natural gas is a coal killer, brings improved air quality and reduced greenhouse gas emissions, and can aid rather obstruct the development and deployment of zero-carbon energies.

The coal-to-gas switch is not inevitable. Concerns about the environmental impacts of natural gas have kept shale fracking out of New York State and resulted in opposition to expanded natural gas production around the country. Gas production levels flattened in response to low prices; more recently, as such unsustainably low prices have risen, coal has regained some of its lost share in the energy mix. American policy makers will make a series of decisions that directly affect the pace of the global and American transition to natural gas. These decisions should be made with an eye to reducing the negative side effects of gas production, increasing production and consumption of gas, and reducing the production and consumption of coal—three goals that are consonant with both improved environmental quality and economic growth.

This report evaluates the key claims and counterclaims made about the environmental impact of natural gas production, and comes to the following conclusions.

1. The climate benefits of natural gas are real and are significant.

Recent lifecycle assessments studies confirm that natural gas has just half as much global warming potential as coal. The evidence suggests that the lower carbon intensity of natural gas far outweighs the warming caused by today's level of methane leakage. Methane is about 20 times more potent as a greenhouse gas than CO_2 on a 100-year basis, and about 70 times more potent on a 20-year basis. Early estimates of methane leakage at levels approaching 7 percent were outliers, and the best estimates of average leakage rates range between 1 and 2 percent. Additionally, methane leakage can be managed and will continue to decline as stricter state regulations enter into force and as the industry moves toward better well completion practices, better compliance with other best practices, and continued technological innovation.

It is not the case that reduced US coal consumption has been offset by increased exports of US coal. From 2008 to 2012, annual coal consumption for US electric power declined, on average, by 50 million tons. Over the same four years, annual exports increased by only 14.5 million tons on average.

2. Cheap gas helps rather than undermines the development and deployment of zero-carbon energy sources like solar and wind, and does not significantly add to the challenges facing the nuclear power industry.

The deployment and overall development of many zero-carbon energy sources—including solar, wind, and nuclear—depends primarily on public policies such as mandates and subsidies, not on the price of natural gas. Rather than being opposed by natural gas, intermittent renewables like solar and wind depend on flexible generation to balance the variability that they introduce into the grid. Natural gas-fired power plants are ideally suited to this task. At present there are few scalable and inexpensive grid-scale storage options, which is why flexible, gas-fired power plants are critical to integrating large volumes of variable solar and wind farms. The corollary to this is that renewables tend not to displace nonvariable base load sources of energy like coal and nuclear, more often replacing natural gas. If it weren't for natural gas' flexible generation, renewables would have far less value as increasing contributors to the electricity grid.

The nuclear power industry has long faced numerous unique obstacles, including a complex regulatory process, lengthy construction times, high capital costs, frequent cost overruns, and public skepticism. The challenges faced by the nuclear industry, especially the building of new plants, are made marginally more difficult by the ongoing natural gas revolution. However, gas's impacts on nuclear pale in comparison to its impacts on coal, and the long-term imperatives for nuclear power—technological innovation, modularization and standardization of design, and cost reduction—are not changed by the arrival of cheap natural gas.

With much of the world's fossil resources expected to be extracted and burned in the coming decades, experts agree that carbon capture technologies will prove to be an essential component of technological portfolios to mitigate climate change. While carbon capture and sequestration technologies (CCS) are often considered in the context of new and existing coal-fired power, there are reasons to expect that CCS will be more easily developed and deployed with natural gas plants. The cleaner stream of emissions from natural gas combustion and the lower capital costs of gas plants make CCS retrofits and demonstrations attractive options for carbon mitigation.

The claim that new natural gas plants are a "sunk investment" and slow the transition to zero-carbon energy sources is undermined by the low-capital costs of gas electricity. The capital costs of new coal, nuclear, and renewable (wind, solar, geothermal, and biomass) power plants are typically several times greater than those of gas plants. In contrast to these other sources, the greatest cost of natural gas is the fuel, not the equipment. Variable operation and fuel costs can be as much as 70 percent of the total levelized cost of a natural gas power plant. By comparison, variable costs for new coal and nuclear plants are, respectively, only about 30 percent and 10 percent of the total levelized cost.

Finally, the low prices created by the shale gas revolution have generated more than $100 billion in energy cost savings every year since at least 2009, giving strong justification to critical subsidies and R&D investments by the Department of Energy starting in the early 1970s. The unconventional gas boom also generated $31 billion in state and federal revenues in 2012, revenues that are expected to grow to over $55 billion by 2025. By 2015, the additional wealth added to the American economy by the shale gas revolution will alone have exceeded the cost of all federal energy subsidies between 1950 and 2012.

3. Natural gas production generally and shale fracturing specifically have a far smaller impact on mortality and disease, landscapes, waterways, air pollution, and local communities than coal mining and coal burning.

This is not to say that there are no real hardships experienced by communities and individuals or negative environmental impacts from the expansion of natural gas production. There are, and they should be proactively confronted. But making a normative judgment about energy policy requires asking whether the impacts of gas production are more or less than the impacts of the fuel it is replacing, principally coal.

The environmental and community impacts of shale fracking are reliably far more modest than those created by coal mining and production. Whereas coal mining removes entire mountains and contaminates streams with hazardous waste, natural gas drill pads occupy only a few hundred square feet, and there are only a handful of cases of groundwater contamination by fracking chemicals. Whereas innovation in coal mining resulted in greater landscape degradation, innovation in gas fracking has resulted in less-toxic fracking chemicals, fewer drill pads, and better drilling practices.

Accelerating the shift from coal to natural gas should be one of the highest energy policy priorities of policymakers and the public. The revolution in shale fracturing and mapping technologies opens up the possibility for developed and developing countries alike to radically reduce consumption of coal in ways that accelerate rather than slow economic growth. Natural gas that is cheaper than coal makes it easier for the Environmental Protection Agency to impose more-stringent air pollution regulations on coal power plants. And cheap natural gas boosts higher rates of economic growth and national wealth to invest in developing its eventual zero-carbon replacements.

Recommendations

Accelerate the coal-to-gas shift in the United States.

Better state regulations and industry oversight should be encouraged to continuously improve the environmental performance of gas drilling, and to address public concerns about pollution and noise. Such efforts will help lay the groundwork for expanded natural gas production on public and private lands. Policymakers should also support the export of liquefied natural gas, which will provide greater price stability, helping the industry avoid the boom-bust cycle that stalled gas production in 2012. Policymakers should also consider including natural gas in any future clean energy standards.

Reduce coal consumption and coal exports.

The Obama administration should pursue stronger pollution and carbon dioxide regulations to make coal increasingly expensive and incentivize the switch to natural gas. Policymakers should support policies that would leave US coal in the ground, rather than mining it for export to Europe and Asia. There will be no net environmental benefit if all of the coal that the US was going to burn for its domestic electricity is exported abroad. US policymakers could reduce global coal supplies and encourage gas production by restricting and eventually halting all US coal exports.

Export natural gas technologies to coal-dependent countries.
The US and global development institutions should promote gas exploration in other countries in ways that accelerate economic development and improve local environmental quality. Such an effort would align United Nations energy access goals with US and international climate goals. It would help China, India, South Africa, and other developing nations to reduce air pollution and meet growing energy demand. And it would help diversify the number of energy exporters around the globe, reducing some of the geopolitical risks associated with geographically disproportionate energy reserves.

Pay it forward.
The shale gas revolution has contributed more than $100 billion to the economy every year since 2009 in the form of lower energy prices. Within five years the economic benefits from shale gas alone will pay for all US energy subsidies since 1950. The critical role that US subsidies played in enabling the shale gas revolution, and its extraordinary economic benefits, suggests that policymakers should make long-term investments in innovation of renewables and nuclear energy. The rapid gas revolution in the United States demonstrates the effects of sustained public-private technology investments, providing a model of a successful energy transition for zero-carbon options like renewables and nuclear.

Fracking Is Helpful in the Short Term

Alison Singer

Alison Singer is pursuing a master's degree in Environmental Policy and Politics at Appalachian State University, after which she hopes to work in the climate policy field.

As the world hurtles towards catastrophic climate change, it is imperative to evaluate current policies, implement new policies, and transition towards a planet less dependent on fossil fuels. Easily accessible fossil fuels have been depleted due to our dependence on them, and hydraulic fracturing (fracking) has been touted as a way to increase extraction efficiency and help sustain our current energy consumption rates. However, fracking has also been roundly criticized as environmentally damaging, and as a simple band-aid strategy to delay the inevitable end of fossil fuels.

Fracking is a way to increase the efficiency of oil and gas wells, as well as access previously untapped reserves, and is performed by pumping fracturing fluid (composed of water, chemicals, and materials to keep the induced fracture open) into a wellbore. Fracking has been most developed in the United States, where it has contributed to increased oil and natural gas production for several years. Shale gas in particular has been heralded as an energy revolution—shale gas has grown from 2% of U.S. gas production in 2000 to 40% in 2012, and is touted as a substantially cleaner alternative to coal.

Thomas Friedman, author of *Hot, Flat, and Crowded*, agrees that fracking should be exploited, as it is much cleaner than coal, and inexpensive to disseminate. However, he is clear about the environmental dangers of fracking, including large amounts of methane leakage. Methane is even more dangerous than carbon dioxide in terms of its atmospheric warming properties. Friedman

"Fracking: The Solution? Or the Problem?" by Alison Singer, March 4, 2013. Reprinted by permission

suggests that we regulate fracking, ensuring the environment is as protected as it can be. At the same time he warns that fracking must not be relied upon in any long-term plans. It is imperative to continue developing renewable energy technologies, and providing the political and economic incentives to implement such technologies. Fracking should be used on a short-term basis only, while we quickly transition to a sustainable, renewable energy future.

Thomas Princen, Jack P. Manno, and Pamela Martin explore this possible new future in their State of the World 2013 chapter, "Keep Them in the Ground: Ending the Fossil Fuel Era." They understand that we live in a world built by fossil fuels, and we cannot simply ignore the energy potential of fossil fuels, but in order to prevent catastrophic climate change, we must utilize that potential as a springboard towards a world where renewable energy drives society. Fossil fuels must be strictly regulated and used only when a substitute cannot be found. Instead of racing to uncover hidden reservoirs of fossil fuels, the authors argue that we must "imagine a deliberately chosen post-fossil fuel world," and then act in such a way to make that dream a reality.

However, it is difficult for many to ignore the immediate economic benefits to fracking. Boomtowns have arisen in congruence with the increased emphasis on fracking, and some of the most depressed parts of the United States now have unemployment rates below 1%, providing high-paying jobs to thousands of workers. Fracking has the potential to provide energy independence, a transition to cleaner energy, and economic prosperity to regions rich in untapped natural resources. However, it also poses dangerous risks to the environment, and may increase our dependence on fossil fuels instead of helping the transition to renewable energy and a cleaner future.

From an environmental perspective, fracking poses a number of risks. Millions of gallons of water are pumped underground, and in places that already suffer from water shortages, this will only add to the problem. Chemicals are mixed with the water, and multiple studies have shown that these chemicals may contaminate groundwater. In addition to massive water usage and groundwater contamination, fracking has also been linked to increases in seismic activity.

Indeed, many areas have banned fracking in response to public outcries and environmental concern. In 2011 France became the first country to ban fracking, and lawmakers have vowed to uphold the ban until it can be proven that fracking definitively does not lead to groundwater contamination. Quebec has also instituted a fracking moratorium, as have several states in the United Stated, as a result of increased public pressure. Reports of increased earthquake activity, illnesses in livestock exposed to fracking fluid, and fears of groundwater contamination have prompted protests and legal action across the globe.

But the most dangerous aspect of fracking is the perpetuation of our fossil fuel dependence. Though fracking offers access to more fuel, and increases extraction efficiency in difficult wells, it is still concerned with a finite, polluting resource. Burning natural gas releases fewer carbon emissions than does burning coal, but this benefit may be offset by high methane leakage from gas fields. Additionally, shifting from coal to natural gas simply shifts our reliance from one fossil fuel to another. Though many fracking proponents claim that natural gas can provide the United States with 100 years of energy, this claim has been slashed to only 24 years, and that assumes no huge leaps in consumption. While we have built a society on fossil fuels, it is becoming increasingly obvious that we cannot sustain such a society for very much longer—not if we hope to prevent dramatic disruptions in human society caused by temperature increases of 4 or even more degrees Celsius. Thus we're going to need strong commitments to policies that get us toward a sustainable future, one where the use of fossil fuels and their effects on the climate is considered seriously.

In order to provide measurement standards and promote better policy making, the Sustainable Governance Indicators (SGI) project has evaluated 31 OECD states, many of which are among the world's top polluters, in terms of their environmental protection. The overarching question they ask is whether current policies protect and preserve resources and the quality of the environment. SGI uses six indicators to compile an overall score: policy rhetoric and implementation, energy intensity, CO_2 emissions, renewable energy, water usage, and waste management.

Overall, Nordic states scored highest, with waste management being the most pervasive problem, and proposed increases in nuclear energy causing some controversy. States with lower scores often demonstrate policy failures or political gridlock. For example, France abandoned its carbon tax and South Korea lowered its gas tax. Additionally, many states continue to have high CO_2 emissions and a lack of incentives for renewable energy. The SGI's analysis points to some serious problems in current environmental policies, and is indicative of the global difficulty to lower emissions and fossil fuel dependence. But it also offers some insight into how we might solve, or at least bypass, these problems and move towards a more renewable, sustainable society.

Coal Seam Gas Can Provide Australia With Clean Energy

Dennis Cooke

Dennis Cooke is Program Manager for Unconventional Resources at the Australian School of Petroleum, University of Adelaide. He has more than 25 years of experience in the oil and gas industry.

In a coal-abundant nation trying to go green, coal seam gas drilling offers us a cleaner source of energy.

But there is a draw back.

Many coal seam wells will require fraccing and the community is concerned about water supply contamination with unknown and potentially toxic frac chemicals, environmental disturbance and adequate regulation.

So how can we get the most out of our natural gas supplies and protect the environment?

Natural gas: why we should make the switch

The natural gas produced from coal seam gas wells is a cleaner alternative to brown coal: it generates about half the amount of CO_2.

Eastern Australia generates most of its electricity from coal—and most of that is emissions-intensive brown coal.

The potential of natural gas as an energy source is huge.

It has been estimated that Australia could meet its Kyoto CO_2 reduction targets just by replacing the large amount of coal we burn for electricity generation with natural gas.

So eastern Australia could switch from coal to natural gas and lessen its impact on the climate and environment. But coal is cheaper than natural gas so, for now, we burn coal.

"Switching to Coal seam gas could drastically reduce emissions—so what's the fraccing problem?" by Dennis Cooke, The Conversation, March 28, 2011. https://theconversation.com/switching-to-coal-seam-gas-could-drastically-reduce-emissions-so-whats-the-fraccing-problem-16.

An average coal seam gas well can be drilled in less than a week, produce gas and water for 20-30 years and costs about $2-4 million.

The average well will produce the energy equivalent of 30-50 million litres of petrol, produce a few hundred giga-litres of water and generate hundreds of thousands of dollars in tax revenue. The planned Queensland LNG plants will require between ten and twenty thousand gas wells.

Most of the gas to be extracted from the new proposed coal seam gas wells will be exported to Asia and will not be available to displace coal as an energy source in Australia.

It seems our Asian neighbours value cleaner-burning fuels more than we do.

Tapping the coal seam

To understand the issues surrounding coal seam gas drilling in Australia, it's important understand how gas is stored in coal and how we get it out. It's this process that goes to the heart of community concern about fraccing.

The important facets of coal are the coal bed, the fractures in the coal bed, the 'small' amount of water stored in the coal and the large amount of gas stored in the coal.

In order to get the gas to flow out of the coal, the water must be pumped out first. The water is stored in the coal like water is stored in a sponge.

The volume of water in a coal is approximately 1% of the volume of coal. This may sound like a small amount of water, but one needs to remember that the amount of coal underground is huge.

A single coal seam may be 10 metres thick and extend for tens of kilometers in all directions. One percent of that coal volume corresponds to a huge amount of water.

So the coal seam gas wells are designed to pump this water and gas to the surface. But coal is impermeable—water and gas will not flow through it.

The water and gas can flow through the fractures—if they are open. But for perhaps half of the wells, the fractures are not open.

This is where fraccing comes in. Fraccing will force the closed fractures open using high pressure water—and some chemicals.

Once the fractures are opened, a much greater quantity of water from the coal bed can flow back to the well bore where it is pumped to the surface. As time goes on, the water level and water pressure in the coal drops and the flow rate of gas increases.

Coal seam gas well regulations are supposed to ensure that frac chemicals do not harm the community, gas does not leak from the well and that no water flows in the well into or out of acquifers found between the surface and the coal bed.

Similarly, environmental regulations are supposed to ensure that produced water does not harm the soils, waterways or bore water.

The ghosts of *Gasland*

Community concerns about frac chemicals are a direct result of American regulators giving frac companies permission to keep the mix of chemicals secret.

Those companies did this not because they wanted to hide the fact that these chemical were toxic—but because they felt that their particular mix of chemicals was a competitive advantage that they did not wish to reveal to the public or to competitors.

This strategy backfired and became a public relations nightmare when the American documentary *Gasland* showed a farmer igniting the water coming from his kitchen tap. The implication in *Gasland* is that the farmer's well water had been contaminated with frac chemicals.

The kitchen tap water in *Gasland* ignited because the farmer's well water came from a well drilled into coal. The farmer's well—or other coal seam gas wells—had lowered the water level in his coals and the coals were starting to produce gas.

This is exactly the behaviour expected and observed from thousands of coal seam gas wells in Queensland.

With regard to the toxicity of these chemicals: the frac fluids are 95% water, and the frac companies have always insisted that the remaining 5% chemicals in the frac fluid are safe.

Of course, nobody believes that these 'secret' chemicals are safe—especially after *Gasland*. The frac companies now are struggling to repair their reputation and are happy to reveal what the frac chemicals are.

In fact, some frac companies are considering only using 100% water as a frac fluid—and ensuring that the water meets drinking water quality standards.

As with most energy production, those who live in rural areas are most impacted by coal seam gas activity. Frequently, these people stay in the bush because they prefer a quiet and clean environment.

Coal seam gas production involves frequent trucks, drilling, pipelines, and processing plants, making their bush environment more industrial.

Are there proper regulations in place to protect the rural nature these citizens treasure? Is it reasonable to suppress coal seam gas development, as well as tax dollars and jobs, in an effort to protect the bush lifestyle?

These are very tough, highly political questions the government and regulators need to consider.

It's worth noting, however, that an open pit coal mine, our current energy sourcing default, is more damaging to the landscape than coal seam gas wells and much worse for the environment.

Once the water is pumped from the coal, it can be fresh or it can be very saline (salty). Where it's too salty for irrigation, the water is stored in evaporation ponds.

The worst-case scenario is that important ground wells are contaminated with this saline water. There is a very low chance of this happening but if an accident occured it would be very difficult to detect until after the contamination has happened.

The importance of regulation

If coal seam gas drilling is to be well-regulated, and it's crucial that it is, the question must be asked: do the different state agencies regulating the industry have sufficient manpower?

There has been a huge upswing in activity to assemble plans and obtain permits for wells, pipelines, evaporation ponds and LNG plants, but companies are finding it difficult to find trained personnel to assemble acceptable plans.

Furthermore, the companies usually pay more than state regulatory agencies, and like to hire state regulators and inspectors because they know the regulations.

There's a genuine concern that the state regulators and inspectors are stretched too thin to adequately review plans and inspect wells associated with this boom of coal seam gas activity.

If we're going to take advantage of cleaner energy options, we have to ensure we have the resources and regulations in place to do it safely.

Fracking Does Little to Negate Climate Change

Christine Ottery

Christine Ottery is a writer, feminist, and frequent contributor to the Greenpeace Energydesk.

One of the arguments around shale gas extraction in the UK has been about whether or not it is compatible with the UK's aim of preventing catastrophic climate change by limiting emissions from fossil fuels.

It's not as obvious as it may—at first—appear. The person in charge of the UK's climate and energy policy, Amber Rudd, has said fracking gas is a low carbon source of power—comments that were recently repeated by Labour peer and anti-coal campaigner Bryony Worthington.

The suggestion is that because gas is lower carbon than coal it can play a role in tackling climate change.The problem is that shale gas is obviously not lower carbon compared to renewable technologies such as wind and solar or nuclear. And saying fracked gas is low carbon implies it's a low climate risk, which simply isn't the case, for several reasons:

1) Coal to fracked gas switching in the UK won't happen

Sigh. The argument that gas from fracking can replace our old coal plants in the UK is one we've debunked before.

Assuming that we do take action on climate change to stay within the internationally-agreed 2 degrees threshold—and dodge more severe droughts, floods and storms—fracking will come too late to the party in the UK.

"Factcheck: Is fracking compatible with action on climate change?" by Christine Ottery, Greenpeace, September 30, 2015. http://energydesk.greenpeace.org/2015/09/30/factcheck-is-fracking-compatible-with-action-on-climate-change/.

To stay within 'safe' levels the government's climate advisers, the Climate Change Committee say we really need phase out coal sharpish—by the early 2020s.

Fracking, however, won't be online in commercially significant amounts for another 10-15 years—if it goes ahead. This timing means fracking won't be able to push coal off the system, something a 2015 Environmental Audit Committee report on fracking pointed out in its conclusions.

Even if fracking gas came online sooner, it would likely be in proportionally small amounts and be more expensive than coal—so it wouldn't displace it.

2) Coal to fracked gas switching won't happen in Europe

If you take a wider perspective, fracked gas still won't replace coal. A seminal modeling study published in *Nature* at the start of the year found that we have to keep 78% of known coal reserves in the ground in Europe by 2050 to stay within two degrees—and that's with CCS. Without it that figure rises to 89%.

Whereas we can probably still burn most of our gas reserves in Europe and stay within 2 degrees.

The problem lies in the fact that—as one of the report's authors environmental policy professor and director of UCL's Institute for Sustainable Resources Paul Ekins puts it: "If there were to be considerable unconventional gas extraction in Europe it would need to substitute for other reserves that are burned in our current scenario".

This is because the gas burned in the UCL study scenario does not include European shale gas reserves. This makes sense, because you would expect the cheapest gas to be used first—and fracked gas is more expensive than conventional gas, according to the IEA and Ernst and Young.

3) Fracked gas won't replace coal globally, or Qatari LNG imports

A 2013 government report known as the MacKay report, led by Professor David MacKay, concluded that: "In the absence of global climate policies, we believe it is credible that shale-gas use would increase both short-term and long-term emissions rates."

This is because "The production of shale gas could increase global cumulative GHG emissions if the fossil fuels displaced by shale gas are used elsewhere", in the absence of such an agreement.

As MacKay points out, this shunting of emissions from one place to another is already going on in the US, where the shale gas boom has had a role in reducing domestic demand for coal—but increasing coal exports to other regions.

In fact, we don't just need a global climate agreement- which will be discussed at the Paris climate talks in December and could pave the way for a 2 degrees world—for fracked gas to replace coal globally you would also need whole new international mechanisms.

"You can only use lots of gas while staying within the 2oC limit if it implicitly and explicitly substitutes for coal, and at the moment there are no institutional means to ensure that," Ekins told Energydesk, "any case for sustainably burning new sources of gas needs to say what fossil fuels it will displace, and be clear about compensation arrangements that would need to be put in place if cheaper fossil fuel reserves are to be displaced in other parts of the world."

Similar arguments could be made for shale gas displacing LNG imports from Qatar as displacing coal. LNG from Qatar has a higher carbon intensity than fracked gas is estimated to have according to the chart from MacKay, at right.

But this assumes that 90% of methane released during the process are captured and flared. This 10% that's emitted could be more or less important—evidence is mixed. Studies looking at the methane emissions from fracking in the US vary from saying that they are lower than previously thought to saying they have been grossly underestimated.

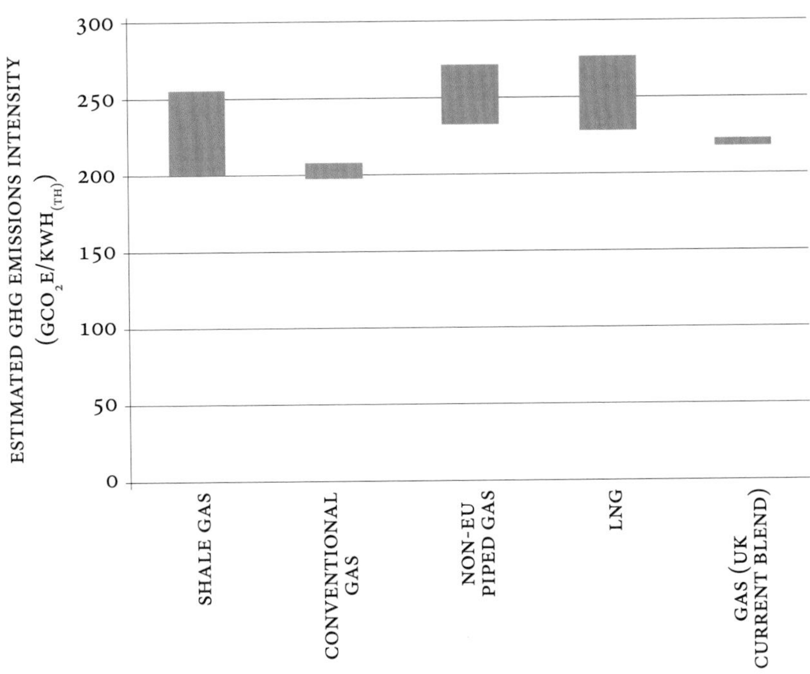

Anyway, if there's no global agreement or mechanism to substitute energy sources, then Qatari LNG will just get burnt elsewhere.

In theory, a global carbon trading system could be a step towards internationally traded emissions allowances—but it's unfeasible and the EU emissions trading system has so far failed to work.

4) If we frack, we could undermine UK climate leadership

John Ashton was the government's special envoy for climate change for six years until 2012, and says climate diplomacy—the very thing that could resolve the issues about displaced emissions—is a good reason not to frack.

In a speech last year he said it would become impossible to ask other countries to leave their conventional reserves in the ground while going "hell for leather to extract unconventional gas and oil from under our own feet.

"We would no longer be listened to," he added.

5) Fracking could detract from investment in renewables

Ashton—who has said people who think we can deal with climate change and frack "are being ignorant, or deceitful, or deceiving themselves"—also argues that even if fracking displaced a little conventional gas in the UK, exploiting unconventional resources would lock us into a dependency on gas—and therefore create a chilling effect on renewables and energy savings investment.

Indeed the evidence from the US shows not only that the shale gas boom was not a major factor in reducing US emissions—as previously thought—but that part of the problem was that shale gas didn't just substitute for coal but also for clean energy.

Ashton's words echo warnings by professors from Harvard and MIT, and UK's The Tyndall Centre. MIT Professor Henry Jacoby, an expert in environmental policy, said: "there had better be something at the other end of the [gas] bridge". Given the current state of UK policy on renewables it's hard to work out what that might be.

6) And no, Carbon Capture and Storage (CCS) isn't a get out of jail free card

Some have argued that all these problems can be overcome if shale gas is only used in circumstances where the carbon emitted is captured and stored someplace underground, for ever.

To start with this suggestion is highly impractical. Much of the gas we use is for domestic heating where this technology can't work.

Of course gas is also used for power generation. But taking shale gas, which is already expensive, and using it to fuel a technology which has been a long time coming and is currently only economically viable if you use it to stimulate oil extraction seems—at best—an odd approach to tackling climate change.

Still if you did want to do this it would be better—from a climate point of view—to burn gas from existing reserves rather than increasing global supply still further while arguing for fossil fuels to be kept in the ground.

Natural Gas Will Not Solve the World's Energy Problems

Gail Tverberg

Gail Tverberg is a researcher and writer at Our Finite World. She studies how energy limits and the economy are interconnected, and what this means for our future.

We keep hearing about the many benefits of natural gas–how burning it releases less CO_2 than oil or coal, and how it burns with few impurities, so does not have the pollution problems of coal. We also hear about the possibilities of releasing huge amounts of new natural gas supplies, through the fracking of shale gas. Reported reserves for natural gas also seem to be quite high, especially in the Middle East and the Former Soviet Union.

But I think that people who are counting on natural gas to solve the world's energy problems are "counting their chickens before they are hatched". Natural gas is a fuel that requires a lot of infrastructure in order for anything to "happen". As a result, it needs a lot of up-front investment, and several years time delay. It also needs changes on the consumption side (requiring further investment) that will allow this natural gas to be used. If the cost is higher than competing fuels, this becomes a problem as well.

In many ways, natural gas consumption is captive to other things that are happening in the economy: an economy that is industrializing rapidly will easily be able to consume more natural gas, but an economy in decline will find it hard to scrape together funds for new ways of doing what was done previously, now with natural gas. Increased use of renewables seems to call for additional use of natural gas for balancing, but even this is not certain, because in many parts of the world, natural gas is a high-priced imported

"Why Natural Gas isn't Likely to be the World's Energy Savior," by Gail Tverberg, October 17, 2012. https://ourfiniteworld.com/2012/10/17/why-natural-gas-isnt-likely-to-be-the-worlds-energy-savior/.

fuel. Political instability, often linked to high oil and food prices, creates a poor atmosphere for new Liquefied Natural Gas (LNG) facilities, no matter how attractive the pricing may seem to be.

In the US, we have already "hit the wall" on how much natural gas can be absorbed into the system or used to offset imports. US natural gas production has been flat since November 2011, based on EIA data.

Even with this level of production, and a large shift in electricity production from coal to natural gas, natural gas is still on the edge of "maxing out" its storage system before winter hits.

World Natural Gas Production

The past isn't the future, but it does give a little bit of understanding regarding what the underlying trends are.

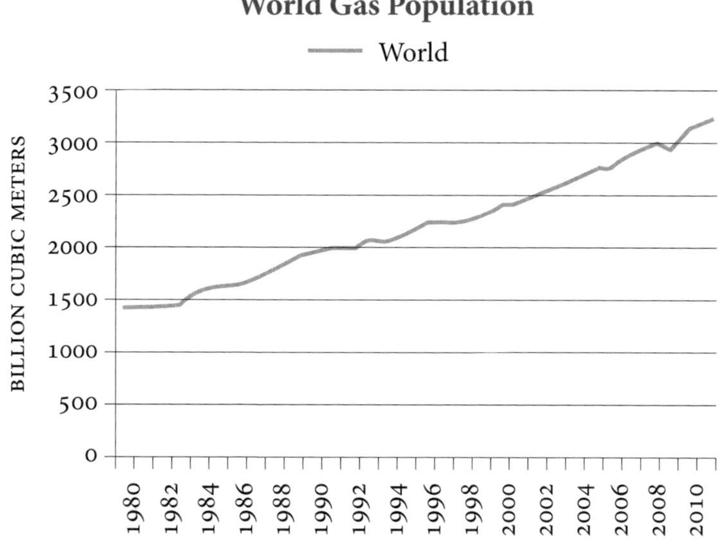

Figure 1. World natural gas production, based on BP's 2012 Statistical Review of World Energy data.

World natural gas production/consumption (Figure 1) has been increasing, recently averaging about 2.7% a year. If we compare natural gas to other energy sources, it has been second to coal in terms of the amount by which it has contributed to the total increase in world energy supplies in the last five years (Figure 2). This comparison is made by converting all amounts to "barrels of oil equivalent", and computing the increase between 2006 and 2011.

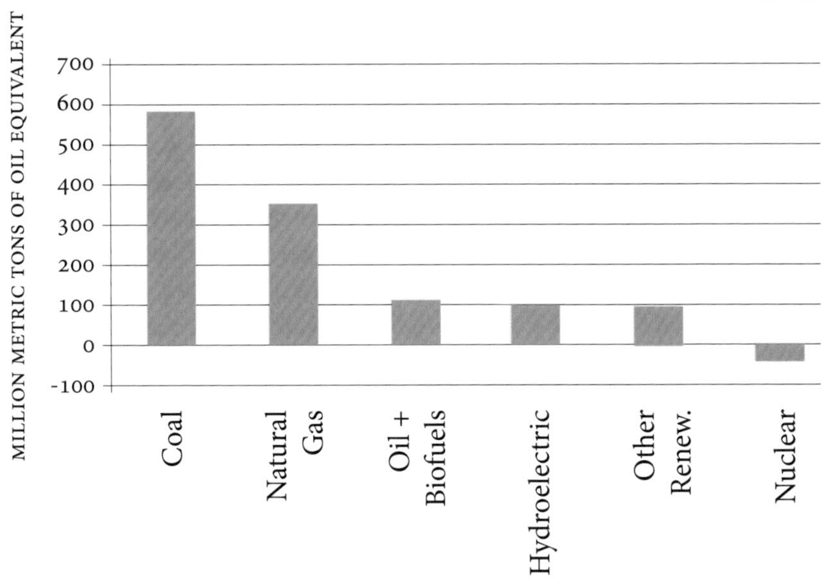

Figure 2. Increase in energy supplied for the year 2011, compared to the year 2006, for various fuels, based on BP's 2012 Statistical Review of World Energy data.

In order for natural gas to be an energy savior for the world, natural gas consumption would need to increase far more than 2.7% per year, and outdistance the increase in coal consumption each year. While a modest increase from past patterns is quite possible, I don't expect a miracle from natural gas.

Natural Gas: What Has Changed?

The basic thing that has changed is that fracking now permits extraction of shale gas (in addition to other types of gas), if other conditions are met as well:

1. Selling price is high enough (probably higher than for other types of natural gas produced)
2. Water is available for fracking
3. Governments permit fracking
4. Infrastructure is available to handle the fracked gas

Even before the discovery of shale gas, reported world natural gas reserves were quite high relative to natural gas production (63.6 times 2011 production, according to BP). Reserves might theoretically be even higher, with additional shale gas discoveries.

In addition, the use of Liquified Natural Gas (LNG) for export is also increasing, making it possible to ship previously "stranded" natural gas, such as that in Alaska. This further increases the amount of natural gas available to world markets.

What Stands in the Way of Greater Natural Gas Usage?

1. Price competition from coal.

One major use for natural gas is making electricity. If locally produced coal is available, it likely will produce electricity more cheaply than natural gas. The reason shale gas recently could be sold for electricity production in the United States is because the selling price for natural gas dropped below the equivalent price for coal. The "catch" was that shale gas producers were losing money at this price (and have since dropped back their production). If the natural gas price increases enough for shale gas to be profitable, electricity production will again move back toward coal.

Many other parts of the world also have coal available, acting as a cap on the amount of fracked natural gas likely to be produced. A carbon tax might change this within an individual country, but those without such a tax will continue to prefer the lower-price product.

2. Growing internal natural gas use cuts into exports.

This is basically the Exportland model issue, raised by Jeffrey Brown with respect to oil, but for natural gas. If we look at Africa's natural gas production, consumption, and exports, this is what we see:

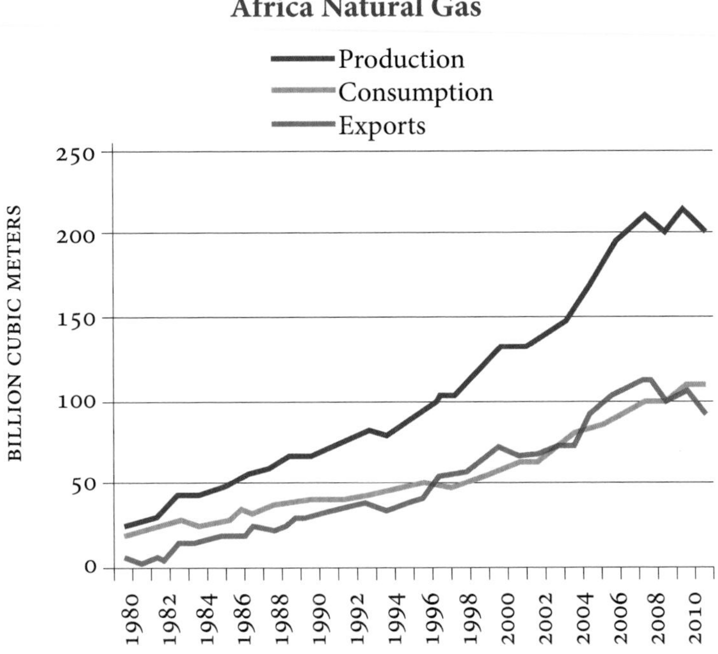

Figure 3. Africa natural gas production, consumption, and exports, based on BP's 2012 Statistical Review of World Energy.

In Africa, (mostly northern Africa, which exports to Europe and Israel), consumption has been rising fast enough that exports have leveled off and show signs of declining.

3. Political instability.

Often, countries with large natural gas resources are ones with large oil resources as well. If oil production starts to drop off, and as a result oil export revenue drops off, a country is likely to experience political instability. A good example of this is Egypt.

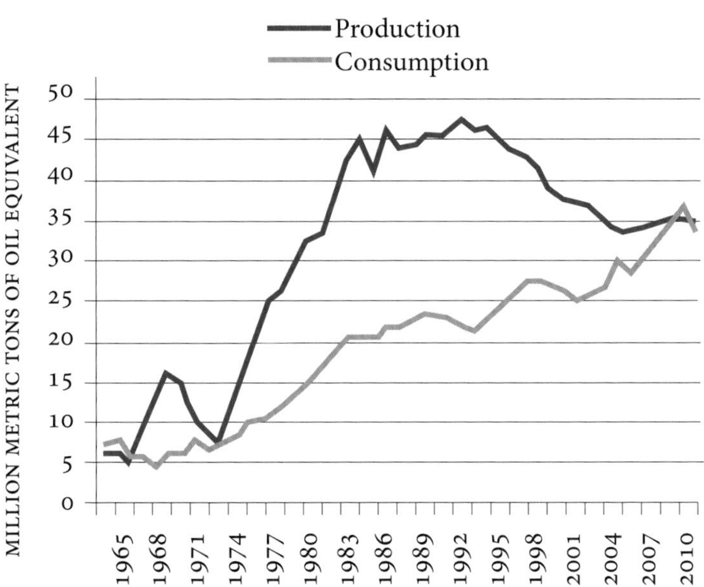

Figure 4. Egypt's oil production and consumption, based on BP's 2012 Statistical Review of World Energy.

No matter how much natural gas Egypt may have, it would not make sense for a company to put in an LNG train or more pipeline export capability, because the political situation is not stable enough. Egypt needs oil exports to fund its social programs. The smaller funding amount available from natural gas exports is not enough to make up that gap, so it is hard to see natural gas making up the gap, even if it were available in significant quantity.

Iran is a country with large natural gas reserves. It is reportedly looking into extractingnatural gas for export. Again, we have a political stability issue. Here we have an international sanctions issue as well.

4. "Need the natural gas for myself later" view.

A country (such as Egypt or the United States or Britain) that has been "burned" by declining oil production may think twice about exporting natural gas. Even if the country doesn't need it now, there is a possibility that vehicles using natural gas could be implemented later, in their own country, thus helping to alleviate the oil shortage. Also, there are risks and costs involved with fracking, that they may not choose to incur, if the benefit is to go to exporters.

5. Cost of investment for additional natural gas consumption.
In order to use more natural gas, considerable investment is needed. New pipelines likely need to be added. Homeowners and businesses may need to purchase gas-fired furnaces to raise demand. If it is decided to use natural gas vehicles, there is a need for the new vehicles themselves, plus service stations and people trained to fix the new vehicles. Additional natural gas storage may be needed as well. Additional industrial production is difficult to add, unless wages are low enough that the product being sold will be competitive on the world market.

Existing "pushes" toward better insulation have the effect of reducing the amount of natural gas used for heating homes and businesses, so work in the opposite direction. So do new techniques for making nitrogen-based fertilizer using coal, rather than using natural gas.

6. Touchy balance between supply and consumption.
If additional production is added, but additional uses are not, we have already seen what happens in the United States. Storage facilities get overly full, the price of natural gas drops to unacceptably low levels, and operators scramble to cut back production.

The required balance between production and consumption is very "touchy". It can be thrown off by only a few percent change in production or consumption. Thus an unusually warm winter, as the United States experienced last year, played a role in the overly full storage problem. A ramp up of production of only a few percent can also cause an out of balance situation. Unless a developer has multiple buyers for its gas, or a "take or pay" long-term contract, it risks the possibility that the gas that is has developed will not be wanted at an adequate price.

7. Huge upfront investment requirements.

There are multiple requirements for investing in new shale gas developments. Each individual well costs literally millions of dollars to drill and frack. The cost will not be paid back for several years (or perhaps ever, if the selling price is not high enough), so debt financing is generally needed. If fracking is done, a good supply of water is needed. This is likely to be a problem in dry countries such as China. There is a need for trained personnel, drilling rigs of the right type, and adequate pipelines to put the new gas into. While these things are available in the United States, it likely will take years to develop adequate supplies of them elsewhere. All of the legislation that regulates drilling and enables pipeline building, needs to be in place as well. Laws need to be friendly to fracking, as well.

Growth in Exports to Date

Exports grew as a percentage of natural gas use through about 2007 or 2008.

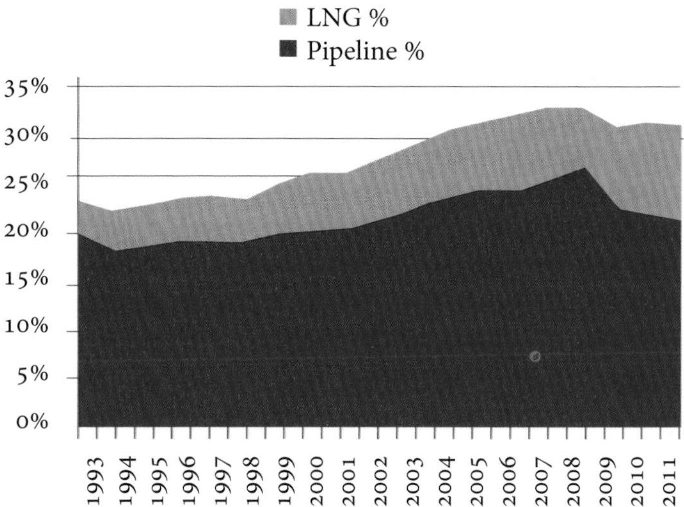

Figure 5. World natural gas exports as percentage of total natural gas produced, by year, based on EIA data (older years) and BP's 2102 Statistical Review of World Energy for 2010 and 2011.

In recent years, natural gas exports have fallen slightly as a percentage of total gas extracted. Thus, if world natural gas supplies have risen by an average of 2.7% per year for the past five years, exports available for import have risen a little less rapidly than the 2.7% per year increase. A major ramp-up in export capability would be needed to change this trend.

While we hear a lot about the rise in exports using LNG, its use does not seem to be adding to the overall percentage of natural gas exported. Instead, there has been a shift in the type of export capacity being added. There are still a few pipelines being added (such as the Nord Stream pipline, from Russia to Germany), but these are increasingly the exception.

The Shale Gas Pricing Debate

Exactly what price is needed for shale gas to be profitable is subject to debate. Shale gas requires the payment of huge up-front costs. Once they are drilled and "fracked," they will produce for a long period. Company models assume that they will last as long as 40 years, but geologist Arthur Berman of The Oil Drum claims substantial numbers are closed down in as few as six years, because they are not producing enough natural gas to justify their ongoing costs. There is also a question as to whether the best locations are drilled first.

Logically a person would expect shale gas to be quite a bit more expensive to produce than other natural gas because it is trapped in much smaller pores, and much more force is required to extracted it. It epitomizes the low quality, hard to extract resource that is available in abundance. We usually extract the easiest and cheapest to extract first.

Berman claims that prices $8.68 or higher per million Btu are needed for profitability of Haynesville Shale, and nearly as high prices are needed to justify drilling other US shale plays. The current US price is about $3.50 per million Btu, so to be profitable, the price would need to be more than double the current US price. Prices for natural gas in Europe are much higher, averaging

$11.08 per million Btu in September 2012, but shale gas extraction costs may be higher there as well.

The US Energy Information Administration admits it doesn't know how the economics will work out, and gives a range of projected prices. It is clear from the actions of the natural gas industry that current prices are a problem. According to Baker Hughes, the number of drilling rigs engaged in natural gas drilling has dropped from 936 one year ago to 422, for the week ended October 12, 2012.

Backup for Renewables

One area where natural gas excels is as a back up for intermittent renewable energy, since it can ramp up and down quickly. So this is one area where a person might expect growth. Such a possibility is not certain, though:

1. How much will intermittent renewables continue to ramp up? Governments are getting poorer, and have less funds available to subsidize them. They do not compete well on when they go head to head with fossil fuels, nuclear, and hydroelectric.
2. When intermittent renewables are subsidized with feed in tariffs, and requirements that wind power be given priority over fossil fuels, it can provide such an unlevel playing field that it is difficult for natural gas to be profitable. This is especially the case in locations where natural gas is already higher-priced than coal.

The Societal "Recipe" Problem

Our economy is built of many interdependent parts. Each business is added, taking into account what businesses already are in place, and what laws are in effect. Because of the way the economy currently operates, it uses a certain proportion of oil, a certain proportion of natural gas, and more or less fixed proportions of other types of energy. The number of people employed tends to vary, too, with the size of the economy, with a larger economy demanding more employees.

Proportions of businesses and energy use can of course change over time. In fact, there is some flexibility built in. In particular, in the US, we have a surplus of natural gas electricity generating units, installed in the hope that they would be used more than they really are, and the energy traded long distance. But there is less flexibility elsewhere. The cars most people drive use gasoline, and the only way to cut back is to drive less. Our furnaces use a particular fuel, and apart from adjusting the temperature setting, or adding insulation, it is hard to make a change in this. We only make major changes when it comes time to sell a car, replace a furnace, or add a new factory.

In my view, the major issue the world has been dealing with in recent years is an inadequate supply of cheap oil. High priced oil tends to constrict the economy, because it causes consumers to cut back on discretionary spending. People in discretionary industries are laid off, and they tend to also spend less, and sometimes default on their loans. Governments find themselves in financial difficulty when they collect fewer taxes and need to pay out more in benefits. While this issue is still a problem in the US, the government has been able to cover up this effect up in several ways (ultra low interest rates, a huge amount of deficit spending, and "quantitive easing"). The effect is still there, and pushing us toward the "fiscal cliff."

The one sure way to ramp up natural gas usage is for the economy as a whole to grow. If this happens, natural gas usage will grow for two reasons: (1) The larger economy will use more gas, and (2) the growth in the economy will add more opportunities for new businesses, and these new businesses will have the opportunity to utilize more natural gas, if the price is competitive.

I have compared the situation with respect to limited oil supply as being similar to that of a baker, who is trying to bake a batch of cookies that calls for two cups of flour, but who has only one cup of flour. The baker is able to make only half a batch. Half of the other ingredients will go unused as well, because the batch is small.

To me, discovering that we have more natural gas than we had before, is analogous to the baker discovering that instead of having a dozen eggs in his refrigerator, there are actually two dozen in his refrigerator. In fact, he finds he can even go and buy more eggs, if he is willing to pay double the price he is accustomed to paying. But the eggs really do not fix the missing cup of flour problem, unless someone can find a way to change eggs into flour very cheaply.

Basic Energy Types

To me, the most basic forms of energy resources are (1) coal and (2) oil. Both can be transported easily, if it is possible to extract them. Natural gas is very much harder to transport and store, so it is in many ways less useful. It can be made work in combination with oil and coal, because the use of coal and oil make it possible to build pipelines and make devices to provide compression to the gas. With coal and oil, it is also possible to make and maintain electric transmission lines to transport electricity made with natural gas.

I sometimes talk about renewable energy being a "fossil fuel extender," because they hopefully make fossil fuels "go farther". In some ways, I think natural gas is an extender for oil and coal. It is hard to imagine a society powered only by natural gas, because of the difficulties in using it, and the major changes required to use it exclusively.

In the earliest days, natural gas was simply a "waste product" of oil extraction. It was "flared" to get rid of it. In many parts of the world, natural gas is still flared, because the effort it takes to collect it, transport it, and make it into a useful product is still too high.

The hope that natural gas will be the world's energy savior depends on our ability to make this former waste product into a product that will replace oil and coal. But unless we can put together an economy that needs and uses it, most of it probably will be left in the ground. The supposedly very high reserves will do us no good.

The Energy Industry Downplays the Many Dangers of Fracking

Reynard Loki

Reynard Loki is AlterNet's environment editor.

With the recent confirmation by the U.S. government that the fracking process causes earthquakes, the list of fracking's deadly byproducts is growing longer and more worrisome. And while the process produces jobs and natural gas, the host of environmental, health and safety hazards continues to make fracking a hot-button issue that evenly divides Americans.

To help keep track of all the bad stuff, here's a roundup of the various nasty things that could happen when you drill a hole in the surface of the earth, inject toxic chemicals into the hole at a high pressure and then inject the wastewater deep underground.

But first, let's take a look at some of the numbers:

- 40,000: gallons of chemicals used for each fracturing site
- 8 million: number of gallons of water used per fracking
- 600: number of chemicals used in the fracking fluid, including known carcinogens and toxins such as lead, benzene, uranium, radium, methanol, mercury, hydrochloric acid, ethylene glycol and formaldehyde
- 10,000: number of feet into the ground that the fracking fluid is injected through a drilled pipeline
- 1.1 million: number of active gas wells in the United States
- 72 trillion: gallons of water needed to run current gas wells
- 360 billion: gallons of chemicals needed to run current gas wells
- 300,000: number of barrel of natural gas produced a day from fracking

"8 Dangerous Side Effects of Fracking That the Industry Doesn't Want you to hear about," by Reynard Loki, Independent Media Institute, April 28, 2015. Reprinted by permission. Reynard Loki, Environment Editor, AlterNet.

And here are eight of the worst side effects of fracking you don't hear about from those slick TV commercials paid for by the industry.

1. Burning the furniture to heat the house.

During the fracking process, methane gas and toxic chemicals leach out from the well and contaminate nearby groundwater. The contaminated water is used for drinking water in local communities. There have been over 1,000 documented cases of water contamination near fracking areas as well as cases of sensory, respiratory and neurological damage due to ingested contaminated water.

In 2011, the *New York Times* reported that it obtained thousands of internal documents from the EPA, state regulators and fracking companies, which reveal that "the wastewater, which is sometimes hauled to sewage plants not designed to treat it and then discharged into rivers that supply drinking water, contains radioactivity at levels higher than previously known, and far higher than the level that federal regulators say is safe for these treatment plants to handle."

A single well can produce more than a million gallons of wastewater, which contains radioactive elements like radium and carcinogenic hydrocarbons like benzene. In addition, methane concentrations are 17 times higher in drinking-water wells near fracking sites than in normal wells. Only 30-50 percent of the fracturing fluid is recovered; the rest is left in the ground and is not biodegradable.

"We're burning the furniture to heat the house," said John H. Quigley, former secretary of Pennsylvania's Department of Conservation and Natural Resources. "In shifting away from coal and toward natural gas, we're trying for cleaner air, but we're producing massive amounts of toxic wastewater with salts and naturally occurring radioactive materials, and it's not clear we have a plan for properly handling this waste."

2. Squeezed out.

More than 90 percent of the water used in fracking well never returns to the surface. Since that water is permanently removed from the natural water cycle, this is bad news for drought-afflicted or water-stressed states, such as Arkansas, California, Kansas, New Mexico, Oklahoma, Utah, Texas and Wyoming.

"We don't want to look up 20 years from now and say, 'Oops, we used up all our water,'" said Jason Banes of the Boulder, Colorado-based Western Resource Advocates.

The redirection of water supplies to the fracking industry not only causes water price spikes, but also reduces water availability for crop irrigation.

"There is a new player for water, which is oil and gas," said Kent Peppler, president of the Rocky Mountain Farmers Union. "And certainly they are in a position to pay a whole lot more than we are."

3. Bad for babies.

The waste fluid left over from the fracking process is left in open-air pits to evaporate, which releases dangerous volatile organic compounds (VOCs) into the atmosphere, creating contaminated air, acid rain and ground-level ozone.

Exposure to diesel particulate matter, hydrogen sulfide and volatile hydrocarbons can lead to a host of health problems, including asthma, headaches, high blood pressure, anemia, heart attacks and cancer.

It can also have a damaging effect on immune and reproductive systems, as well as fetal and child development. A 2014 study conducted by the Colorado Department of Environmental and Occupational Health found that mothers who live near fracking sites are 30 percent more likely to have babies with congenital heart defects.

Research from Cornell University indicates an increased prevalence of low birth weight and reduced APGAR scores in infants born to mothers living near fracking sites in Pennsylvania. And in Wyoming's Sublette County, the fracking boom has been linked to dangerous spikes in ozone concentrations. A study led by the state's Department of Health found that these ozone spikes are associated with increased outpatient clinic visits for respiratory problems.

4. Killer gas.

A recent study by researchers at Johns Hopkins University found that homes located in suburban and rural areas near fracking sites have an overall radon concentration 39 percent higher than those located in non-fracking urban areas. The study included almost 2 million radon readings taken between 1987 and 2013 done in over 860,000 buildings from every county, mostly homes.

A naturally occurring radioactive gas formed by the decay of uranium in rock, soil and water, radon—odorless, tasteless and invisible—moves through the ground and into the air, while some remains dissolved in groundwater where it can appear in water wells. It is the second leading cause of lung cancer worldwide, after smoking. The EPA estimates approximately 21,000 lung cancer deaths in the U.S. are radon-related.

"Between 2005-2013, 7,469 unconventional wells were drilled in Pennsylvania. Basement radon concentrations fluctuated between 1987-2003, but began an upward trend from 2004-2012 in all county categories," the researchers wrote.

That trending period just happens to start when Pennsylvania's fracking boom began: Between Jan. 1, 2005, and March 2, 2012, the Pennsylvania Department of Environmental Protection issued 10,232 drilling permits; only 36 requests were denied.

5. Shifting sands.

In addition to all the water and toxic chemicals, fracking requires the use of fine sand, or frac sand, which has driven a silica sand mining boom in Minnesota and Wisconsin, which together have 164 active frac sand facilities with 20 more proposed. Both states are where most of the stuff is produced and where regulations are lax for air and water pollution monitoring. Northeastern Iowa has also become a primary source.

"Silica can impede breathing and cause respiratory irritation, cough, airway obstruction and poor lung function," according to Environmental Working Group. "Chronic or long-term exposure can lead to lung inflammation, bronchitis and emphysema and produce a severe lung disease known as silicosis, a form of pulmonary fibrosis. Silica-related lung disease is incurable and can be fatal, killing hundreds of workers in the U.S. each year."

"I could feel dust clinging to my face and gritty particles on my teeth," said Victoria Trinko, a resident of Bloomer, Wisconsin. Within nine months of the construction of frac sand mine, about a half-mile from her home, she developed a sore throat and raspy voice and was eventually diagnosed with environment-caused asthma. She hasn't opened her windows since 2012.

Across the 33-county frac sand mining area that spans Minnesota, Wisconsin and Iowa, nearly 60,000 people live less than half a mile from existing or proposed mines. And new danger zones will likely pop up around the nation: Due to the fracking boom, environmentalists and public health advocates warn that frac sand mines could spread to several states with untapped silica deposits, including Illinois, Maine, Massachusetts, Michigan, Missouri, New York, North Carolina, South Carolina, Pennsylvania, Tennessee, Vermont and Virginia.

Bryan Shinn, the chief executive of sand mining company U.S. Silica Holdings said in September that due to the fracking boom, they "see a clear pathway to the volume of sand demand that's out there doubling or tripling in the next four to five years."

6. Shake, rattle and roll.

On April 20, the U.S. Geological Survey released a long-awaited report that confirmed what many scientists have long speculated: the fracking process causes earthquakes. Specifically, over the last seven years, geologically stable regions of the U.S., including parts of Alabama, Arkansas, Colorado, Kansas, New Mexico, Ohio,

Oklahoma and Texas, have experienced movements in faults that have not moved in millions of years. Plus, it's difficult or impossible to predict where future fracking-caused earthquakes will occur.

"They're ancient faults," said USGS geophysicist William Ellsworth. "We don't always know where they are."

Ellsworth led the USGS team that analyzed changes in earthquake occurrence rates in the central and eastern United States since 1970. They found that between 1973–2008, there was an average of 21 earthquakes of at least magnitude three. From 2009-2013, the region experienced 99 M3+ earthquakes per year. And the rate is still rising. In Oklahoma, there were 585 earthquakes in 2014—more than in the last 35 years combined.

"The increase in seismicity has been found to coincide with the injection of wastewater in deep disposal wells in several locations, including Colorado, Texas, Arkansas, Oklahoma and Ohio," the report states. "Much of this wastewater is a byproduct of oil and gas production and is routinely disposed of by injection into wells specifically designed and approved for this purpose."

For many years, Oklahoma's government has been reluctant to concede the connection between fracking and earthquakes. In October of last year, during a gubernatorial election debate with state Rep. Joe Dorman, a Democrat, Governor Mary Fallin, a Republican, declined to say whether or not she believed earthquakes were caused by fracking. Fallin was re-elected.

But the government has finally come around. The day after the USGS report was released, on April 21, the Oklahoma Geological Survey, a state agency, released a statement saying that is it "very likely that the majority of recent earthquakes, particularly those is central and north-central Oklahoma, are triggered by the injection of produced water in disposal wells."

The same day, the state's energy and environment department launched a website that explains the finding along with an earthquake map and what the government is doing about it all. According to the site, "Oklahoma state agencies are not waiting to take action."

Now there is a split between the state's governmental branches: Two days after the executive branch admitted that fracking causes earthquakes, the state's lawmakers, evidently unmoved by the trembling ground, passed two bills, backed by the oil and gas industry, that limit the ability of local communities to decide if they want fracking in their backyards.

7. The heat is on.

Natural gas is mostly methane, a highly potent greenhouse gas that traps 86 times as much heat as carbon dioxide. And because methane leaks during the fracking process, fracking may be worse than burning coal, mooting the claim that natural gas burns more cleanly than coal.

"When you frack, some of that gas leaks out into the atmosphere," writes 350.org co-founder Bill McKibben. "If enough of it leaks out before you can get it to a power plant and burn it, then it's no better, in climate terms, than burning coal. If enough of it leaks, America's substitution of gas for coal is in fact not slowing global warming."

A recent international satellite study on North American fracking production led by the Institute of Environmental Physics at the University of Bremen in Germany found that "fugitive methane emissions" caused by the fracking process "may counter the benefit over coal with respect to climate change" and that "net climate benefit…is unlikely."

"Even small leaks in the natural gas production and delivery system can have a large climate impact—enough to gut the entire benefit of switching from coal-fired power to gas," writes Joe Romm, the founding editor of the blog Climate Progress. "The climate will likely be ruined already well past most of our lifespans by the time natural gas has a net climate benefit."

8. Quid pro quo?

Finally, one of the more insidious side effects of fracking is less about the amount of chemicals flowing into the ground and more about the amount of money flowing into politicians' campaign coffers from the fracking industry.

According to a 2013 report by Citizens for Responsibility and Ethics in Washington (CREW), contributions from fracking trade groups and companies operating fracking wells to congressional candidates representing states and districts where fracking occurs rose by more than 230 percent between the 2004 and 2012 election cycles, from $2.1 million to $6.9 million.

That is nearly twice as much as the increase in contributions from the fracking industry to candidates from non-fracking districts during the same period, outpacing contributions from the entire oil and gas industry to all congressional candidates. Republican congressional candidates have received nearly 80 percent of fracking industry contributions.

"The fracking boom isn't just good for the industry, but also for congressional candidates in fracking districts," said CREW executive director Melanie Sloan.

The candidate who has received the most in contributions from the fracking industry is Rep. Joe Barton (R-TX). Barton received more than $500,000 between the 2004 and 2012 election cycles—over $100,000 more than any other candidate in the nation. It should come as no surprise that Barton sponsored the Energy Policy Act of 2005, which exempted fracking from federal oversight under the Safe Drinking Water Act.

On April 21, Colorado and Wyoming filed a lawsuit challenging the new federal fracking regulations issued last month by the Bureau of Land Management for onshore drilling on tribal and public lands, claiming that the rule, which regulates underground injections in the fracking process, "exceeds the agency's statutory jurisdiction."

"The debate over hydraulic fracturing is complicated enough without the federal government encroaching on states' rights," said Colorado Attorney General Cynthia H. Coffman, in a statement. "This lawsuit will demonstrate that BLM exceeds its powers when it invades the states' regulatory authority in this area."

Coffman, a Republican, is married to Colorado Rep. Mike Coffman (CO-8), also a Republican. Coffman and two other GOP representatives from the state, Scott Tipton (CO-3) and Doug Lamborn (CO-5), have sponsored a trio of bills—H.R. 4321, 4382 and 4383 (called the "3 Stooges" bills by environmentalists)—that would fast-track leasing and permitting for drilling and fracking on public lands. These three congressmen, each of whom have received more than $100,000 in contributions from the oil and gas industry, sit on the Natural Resources Committee and naturally oppose federal regulations on fracking.

Short-Term Thinking

Fracking proponents point to the fact that it produces natural gas and jobs; indeed takes credit for boosting the economy during the recession. But at what cost to public health and the environment? And can the true cost be known when there is a lack of transparency in the fracking industry?

With little federal oversight, states have created a non-uniform patchwork of regulation: Illinois requires fracking companies to disclose information about the chemicals they use before they drill and monitor groundwater through the process, while Virginia doesn't require any disclosure.

"So far, the industry has successfully fended off almost all federal regulation of fracking, in part through key exemptions from federal laws such as the Safe Drinking Water Act, which otherwise would allow the EPA to directly regulate fracking and other aspects of oil and gas production," says CREW.

The FRAC Act (Fracturing Responsibility and Awareness of Chemicals Act) would require the energy industry to disclose all chemicals used in fracturing fluid and also repeal fracking's exemption from the Safe Drinking Water Act.

Of course, everyone wants reliable domestically produced energy that creates jobs and energy independence. But nothing comes for free. And in the case of fracking, still with so many unknowns, the price in the long run may be too great.

That's part of the message that Reps. Mark Pocan (D-WI) and Jan Schakowsky (D-IL) hope the American public gets. On April 22, Earth Day, the two lawmakers introduced the Protect Our Public Lands Act, H.R. 1902. The strongest anti-fracking bill ever introduced into Congress, it seeks to ban fracking on public lands. Today, 90 percent of federally managed lands are open for potential oil and gas leasing; the remaining 10 percent are reserved for conservation, recreation, wildlife and cultural heritage.

"Our national parks, forests and public lands are some of our most treasured places and need to be protected for future generations," said Pocan. "It is clear fracking has a detrimental impact on the environment and there are serious safety concerns associated with these type of wells. Until we fully understand the effects, the only way to avoid these risks is to halt fracking entirely. We should not allow short-term economic gain to harm our public lands, damage our communities or endanger workers."

Sounds logical enough. But with oil and gas money steering the Republican-controlled Congress, the bill is dead in the radioactive wastewater.

Chapter 2

Is Fracking Better for the Environment?

Overview: What Is Fracking's Effect on the Environment?

Steve Rushton

Steve Rushton writes for Occupy.com (US), Debt Resitance UK and has blogged for media platforms including the New Internationalist, Bella Caledonia and the NGO Global Justice Now (formerly World Development Movement). He is interested in many global social justice issues and exploring alternatives; before moving to London and being involved in activism and journalism, he undertook research into the threat of the globalised capitalist world on the indigenous people of Vietnam's Central Highlands.

The decision whether Britain should frack is crucial. The government presents it as the only option. In opposition, a body of evidence suggests it will lead to ecological meltdown. In addition, the current business-as-usual path is creating multiple systemic crises, not least climate change.

Although fracking may boom out across the country 60% of the UK, it is not widely understood. So firstly, what is this unconventional fossil fuel?

What is hydraulic fracturing (fracking)?

The aim of fracking is to extract natural gas from shale that is mostly methane.

In preparation, a rig is erected, under which a borehole or well is dug vertically down to the shale rock, at 1500 metres or deeper. Next, the hole turns horizontally: US fracker Haliburton suggest it can stretch as much as 3,000 metres, running parallel with the surface.

The well is then encased with concrete and steel piping, with perforations or holes in the horizontal sections.

"There Are Alternatives to Fracking," by Steve Rushton, Guardian News and Media Limited, August 2014. Reprinted by permission.

In operation, the process jets millions of gallons of frack-fluid through the pipe, and out of the holes, pressurised at between 10,000-15,000 psi (pounds per square inch). That is similar to the pressure found at the depths of the Mariana Trench, Pacific, the deepest point in the world's oceans. The fluid is water mixed with silica and toxins, including Volatile Organic Compounds, Formaldehyde and Naphthalene.

Fracking involves similar to the pressure found at the depths of the Mariana Trench, Pacific, the deepest point in the world's oceans.

Blasting through the holes in the pipe, the fluid fractures the shale rock to create fissures, air gaps releasing methane and other gases. Haliburton suggests it can recover between 10 to 40% of the fluid back to the surface (known as flowback), the rest is left in the ground. After they have recovered what they can, the gas is extracted.

This fracking process can be repeated until the well is used up; each single frack uses 1 to 8 million gallons of frack-fluid.

Shale gas extraction is relatively new, making it an unconventional fossil fuel. Earlier natural gas extraction still used a rig: but with a vertical borehole. It also did not use the same mixture of frack-fluids or the amounts or pressures of water.

This description explains what should happen. But there are many contentions surrounding the process and its ecological impact. For instance, forerunning UK fracking company Cuadrilla was censured by the Advertising Standards Agency for its claim it uses "proven, safe technologies to explore for and recover natural gas,"

Looking across the Atlantic where the industry has proliferated widely over the last decade, numerous scientific reports, industry admissions and newspaper reports substantiates the strong doubts about the industry's safety.

What are the reported dangers of fracking?

Water contamination

An Associated Press study reports numerous cases of water contamination caused by fracking in Pennsylvania, Ohio, West Virginia, and Texas. Texas has increased levels of arsenic near the industry. Groundwater has been contaminated with cancerous benzene in Colorado. Canadian operations have led to elevated levels of benzene, toluene, ethylbenzene and xylene. All are toxins. Broadly, fracking has been shown to increase levels of radium, substantiated further by a peer-reviewed Duke University paper, which tells how underground radioactivity is unsettled and along with the toxins used threatens human life when it comes to the surface. Another report shows how millions of gallons of flowback are 300 times more radioactive than the limit for nuclear plant discharges.

A Duke University paper asserts pollutants from fracking are a threat to human life.

Pollution can spread through different pathways, such as defects in the well's cement and metal casing. A Connell University study found that 6-7% of wells in Pennsylvania fail. American Shale Oil, whose shareholders include Rupert Murdoch and Dick Cheney has been told it must fix its faulty wells in Colorado. The natural gas industry data suggests 5% of wells leak within 1 year, half within 30, even without the increased pressure and complexities of the fracking process. Underground radioactive materials unsettled by frack-fluid can disperse through rocks, or with toxins and carcinogens travel through subsurface pathways to enter the water cycle.

Accidents and spills are another pollution pathway. Reports from New Mexico show how waste water pits like the one pictured above often overflow or leak. Additionally, there can be too much water to treat as happened in Pennsylvania. Pollution from explosions, over-ground pipeline failures, accidents have been widespread, for instance in North Dakota, Ohio and California.

The *NY Times* reports that residents are more likely to discover leaking over-ground pipelines than the industry.

Evidence shows the industry uses gag orders to silence victims and conceal impacts. They tried to prevent a doctor stating the chemicals in frack-fluids that harmed their patient. Non-disclosure settlements stop homeowners whose water became contaminated speaking publicly. Similarly a case in Texas shows the industry is using intellectual property rules to hide the chemicals from regulators.

Non-disclosure makes it harder to detect pollutants, as regulators do not know what to look for. Problems that can only be exasperated when state officials work to conceal pollution. Concealing information is noted by researchers as a barrier to understanding fracking's total impact.

Water shortages

Amplifying contamination's potential drain on clean water supplies, fracking requires millions of gallons of water. The Guardian tells how fracking has sucked parts of Texas dry. The story is re-told in Denver: frackers there outbids farmers for water. Colorado also faces more droughts. US Environmental Protection Agency figures suggest annually the industry is uses between 70 to 140 billion gallons of water, the same as a city of 2.5 or 5 million inhabitants.

Climate Change

"It is not really that complicated: you can be in favour of fracking for shale gas, or you can be in favour of fixing the climate." John Ashton said at a London panel discussion in June.

He was Special Representative for Climate Change at the UK Foreign Office, 2006-12. The International Panel on Climate Change substantiate this claim, asserting a great deal of conventional fossil fuels needs to be left in the ground to tackle climate change, and no unconventionals (including shale gas) should be extracted. The UN Environmental Programme alerts: "This unconventional gas extraction technique presents environmental risks, despite economic or energy security benefits, including: air, soil, and water contamination; water usage competition; ecosystem damage; habitat and biodiversity impacts; and fugitive gas emissions."

Scientists point to both the energy intensity of the fracking process and that it unleashes methane, seeping out through the same pathways as toxins. It means locals can set fire to their drinking taps. Not only explosive, methane gas is far more potent than CO_2 as a heat-trapping greenhouse gas. Consequently, the levels of methane leaking have led independent scientists to calculate that fracking is worse for the environment than coal, substantiating earlier findings.

Fracking has also been linked to massive rises in ozone pollution in both rural Texas and Wyoming. The latter was known for its crisp mountain air, but has recently recorded smog levels you would expect in large cities. A study in Colorado shows how it increases a further range of dangerous gases that cause acute health problems.

Local impacts: health, ecosystems & agriculture

37 health organisations and a hundred plus medical professionals co-wrote a letter calling for a moratorium on fracking in New York.

It states: "The totality of the science—which now encompasses hundreds of peer-reviewed studies and hundreds of additional reports and case examples—shows that permitting fracking in New York would pose significant threats to the air, water, health and safety of New Yorkers."

More than 100 medics and scientists in New York say fracking causes threats to air, water, health and safety.

The letter suggests fracking of causing numerous health problems, linked to the aforementioned harmful chemicals and radioactive pollution. In Pennsylvania campaigners have compiled a list of 6,000 people harmed or killed due to the industry. A multi-university study has found it endangers babies. Another report shows it can cause infertility, birth defects and cancer. These are among a wide range of serious and often life threatening symptoms, including respiratory problems and neurological impairments that have been reported.

In Pennsylvania, campaigners have compiled a list of 6,000 people harmed or killed by fracking.

The medics' letter asserts there needs to be more extensive research into the impacts of fracking, free from industry's attempts to quash evidence. Likewise in Britain, there are serious questions about whether the industry has funded or is linked to every study that suggests fracking is safe.

In tandem with health, accounts describe that is disastrous for local ecosystems and agriculture. Farmers assert it has killed their livestock and vegetation, including in Pennsylvania, North Dakota and Alberta. The unconventional fossil fuel has also been linked to destroying forests, decimating aquatic life and threatening animals like the antelope of Wyoming.

Increasing fracking has led to claims it intensely industrialises areas in 'gaslands', places immense strain on transport and other infrastructure, leads to work-related deaths, and expands other dangerous industries like mining the carcinogenic silica.

Earthquakes

In 2011, UK fracking operations were halted due to earthquakes, which took Cuadrilla weeks to admit their industry likely caused.

In the area between Alabama, Colorado and Ohio, where fracking is most prolific, insurers note how forty years ago the area averaged 21 earthquakes per year. It rose for the decade before 2011 to 134, that year. Insurers now question whether earthquake insurance will protect against 'man-made-earthquakes'. Consequently, a mayor in Ohio has brought earthquake insurance; in Oklahoma earthquake insurance is a boom industry.

The earthquake insurance business in Oklahoma is now booming.

In stark disagreement, the campaign to frack Britain contradicts these dangers, or argues the industry will achieve higher standards. But to contextualise the case to frack it is relevant to dig into who stands to gain from the unconventional boom of shale, and even who is gaining already.

Who stands to gain from fracking Britain?

Cuadrilla is the lynchpin company in plans to expand fracking across the UK, along with Dart Energy, IGas, Celtique Energy, Egdon Resources and eCorp Oil & Gas. Centrica (formerly British Gas) has bought some licences and Total is the only oil major involved in UK fracking. UK-based companies like Shell have substantial interests in US fracking, although currently they say UK fracking is not viable.

The Conservative government has profited already in donations from fracking interests, revealed by media investigations this year and in 2012. These articles give examples of some of the investors with their money on fracking.

In the mix with donations, there is an often blurred line between the fracking industry and Conservative-led government. Lord Browne is a key example: he is both chairman of Cuadrilla and a senior adviser to the UK government. Senior Conservative advisers Lynton Crosby and Ben Moxham are two other examples. Now advising Cameron, Crosby has fracking interests; Moxham worked for Lord Browne at BP and is now Cameron's energy adviser.

This revolving door spins for state institutions too: news recently broke about Sir Phillip Davies, head of the Environmental Agency. He was Cameron's former adviser and worked for a company producing environmental reports for Cuadrilla. This diagram further maps the fracking-government relations, including Lord Howell George Osborne's father in-law, both peer and fracking lobbyist.

The New Internationalist assert the extent that PR companies are gaining from a frack Britain campaign. In the US, Hill and Knowlton made some of the $80 million spent by the US industry in one campaign. Cuadrilla are employing Bell Pottinger, a firm whose top executives were caught on camera boasting their access to top Tories.

Fracking PR is big business: US Hill and Knowlton profited from a $80 billion shale gas campaign.

Unlike the US, where landowners own mineral rights, British Lord of the Manor rights passed down through the aristocracy gives them the rights to land even if they do not own it. This led to a swathe of reports about how aristocratic landowners were registering these rights to cash-in on fracking. But there is contention this will apply, as under the 1998 Petroleum Act any fossil fuel 'found in strata' belongs to the Queen.

What is clear is that large-scale aristocratic landowners can rent out the areas in which the frack rig is placed. For instance, Simon Greenwood has leased parts of Sussex to enable fracking at Balcombe, in a deal said to make him thousands of pounds.

Whether Britain fracks or not also plays into a wider global debate. Whereas fracking has mainly proliferated across US and Canada, it has been banned or suspended in New York State, Quebec and France. With growing resistance to stop it globally, it is arguable that international fracking interests such as Rupert Murdoch will want fracking to go ahead in the UK to justify its expansion elsewhere.

Some academics and research institutions receive money and sponsorship from the fracking industry. Cuadrilla sponsor academic research including Joe Howe from University of Central Lancashire. They paid him to write a paper about their socio-political impact. Further south, oil company major Shell fund the Shell Geo-Science Laboratory at Oxford University.

There are many more research societies and institutions sponsored by the industry, not least those pushing the case to frack.

The Case to Frack Britain

The government has argued fracking will benefit the whole country and that it can be done safely. A House of Commons paper states: "The health, safety and environmental risks can be managed effectively in the UK, by implementing and enforcing best operational practice."

This relies on evidence from a paper co-authored by the Royal Academy and Royal Society of Engineering. Questions about these conclusions arise though from the latter's direct links and sponsorship from the fracking industry.

The Royal Academy of Engineering is headed by Sir John Parker, whose has fracking interests in South Africa. Its previous chairman was Lord Browne of Cuadrilla. Additionally, it partners with US fracker Exxon-Mobile and independent researchers Corporate Watch site how it receives hundreds of thousands of pounds from frackers.

The aforementioned parliamentary paper asserts fracking has lower emissions than coal, making it a possible 'bridge to a low carbon future'. The science here is from the Department of Climate Change (DECC). Likewise, their objectivity and integrity could be considered dubious. Recent revelations show that Lord Browne oversees appointments at the DECC. Additionally, the government's September 2013 paper relies on data from the British Geological Survey. They receive money from fracking companies: Chevron, ConocoPhillips, Exxon, BG Group and Schlumberger.

Adding to the doubt, the Geological Survey report states how no accurate measurements of the available gas can be made before drilling takes place, in effect any conclusions on the climatic impact are educated guesses.

If sponsoring science can be said to undermine it, this erodes the government's case about earthquakes too. Again they rely on a British Geological Survey to down-plays the risks. A Parliamentary paper tells: "Cuadrilla funded a geo-mechanical study by the BGS which was given to DECC to consider."

Another report that could be viewed as failing an objectivity test is a new report on water contamination. The DECC co-commissioned the British Geological Survey partnering the Natural Environment Research Council (NERC). A body that is guided by an innovation board including senior research executives for Schlumberger Ltd and Shell Global Solutions: two fracking companies. Shell also sponsors NERC research.

With a multitude of independent reports about the severe dangers of fracking, verses reports supported, connected or paid for the industry is seems vital to ask how else we could create energy.

Alternatives to Fracking

The IPCC assertion that fossil fuel business as usual has to stop to avert climate change dovetails with broader ecological argument against fracking—not least its threats to water, ecosystems and human health. A nuclear pathway can be discounted due to its long-term legacy and risks, as shown in Fukushima and Chernobyl. The options left are renewables and energy efficiency.

The global march of renewables

Portugal, for the first 3 months of 2013, produced 70% of its electric power from renewables. Similarly impressive amounts are demonstrated in Germany, which has recently set new laws to reduce fossil fuels and nuclear use.

These examples represent the crest of an eco-energy wave; from Chile's solar power to Iceland, which acquires most of its heating from geo-thermal. In Australia it is cheaper to produce energy from wind than coal or gas. Even in Britain, half a million houses now have solar energy.

These examples show how different countries can benefit from one or more abundant energy sources.

Britain has a range of options: including expanding it already growing wind farms. But possibly, one of the most exciting energy prospects is tidal.

Britain has a range of renewable options, not least expanding wind farms and tidal.

Turning the tide on climate change

Britain has one of the largest global tidal ranges: energy that is predictable and abundant. SeaGen, the single tidal turbine, produces enough energy to supply 1,500 homes.

A Renewables UK report suggests that by 2020, tidal power could generate a significant proportion of Britain's energy needs.

They suggest that what is needed is for the government and media to talk-up the industry to encourage investment; in doing what it is doing for fracking.

Another comparison is that both tidal and fracking are industries in their infancies in Britain. Earlier this year I spoke to Lubo Jankovic, professor of Zero Carbon Design at Birmingham City University. He explained how even if successful, fracking will not be fully operational for 10-20 years. There is a huge controversy about just how long shale gas would last, whereas tidal will never run out.

Energy efficiency and local energy

In tandem with tidal and increasing Britain's other renewables, two other key areas to develop are increasing energy efficiency and local energy schemes.

In an interview earlier this year, researcher Danny Chivers explained how there are 20 million poorly insulated homes in Britain: considerably increasing Britain's energy needs. He told me how the government's schemes are only insulating 400,000 per year, meaning it will take half a century for the country to stop wasting vast quantities of energy.

Chivers has mapped out a two energy futures diagram, which shows how with existing technologies the world could meet its energy needs via renewables.

Local energy production also provides a solution, both to create energy needed for communities and to break the hold of the big energy companies whose priorities are profits not people. In Germany "municipal utilities allow communities to focus on energy efficiency, renewables, and distributed cogeneration without the need for nuclear and coal power." On Scottish islands, community wind farms mean profits from selling energy into the grid are leading to investment in the communities. In a similar renewable vein, a not-for-profit solar cooperative is growing in Brixton, London.

Grow Heathrow, a transition community, shows further local innovations to meet sustainable energy needs. On site they have created plans for a biodigester and gasifying wood burner. Biodigesters may provide a way for communities, streets or tower blocks to turn their organic waste into natural gas. The gasifying woodburner is a way for efficiently heating water from wood.

Any transition to an ecological future would take investment, in terms of human energy, time and expertise. Currently, this investment is being pushed into fossil fuels, including through pension pots. It seems illogical that many workers are putting money to financially secure their retirements, whilst their investments are actively working to endanger the planet they will retire into.

Looking to the future, there are alternatives to fracking that do not threaten air, water and soil; these will take a considerable amount of humanpower to realise. But the real test will be to challenge powers-that-be who are driving us towards a fracked future.

There are alternatives to fracking that do not threaten air, water and soil.

Methane Leaks From Fracking Is a Technical Problem We Can Solve

Roger Real Drouin

Roger Real Drouin is a journalist who covers environmental issues. His articles have appeared in Grist.org, Mother Jones, The Atlantic Cities, and other publications.

Loose pipe flanges. Leaky storage tanks. Condenser valves stuck open. Outdated compressors. Inefficient pneumatic systems. Corroded pipes.

Forty separate types of equipment are known to be potential sources of methane emissions during the production and processing of natural gas and oil by hydraulic fracturing, or fracking, of underground shale formations. As the fracking boom continues unabated across the U.S., scientists, engineers, and government experts are increasingly focusing on the complex task of identifying the sources of these methane leaks and devising methods to stop them.

"There are many, many, many possible leaking sources," said Adam Brandt, a Stanford University professor of energy resources engineering who compiled recent estimates of the oil and gas industry's methane emissions. "Just like a car, there are a variety of ways it can break down."

Even among industry officials, there is agreement that getting control of methane emissions is an important issue. At heart it is an engineering problem, and solutions from government, industry, and academia are beginning to take shape. Analysts say that battling the problem must occur on two closely related fronts: tighter regulations at the state and federal level, and a commitment

"On Fracking Front, A Push To Reduce Leaks of Methane," by Roger Real Drouin, Yale University, April 7, 2014. This article was first published in Yale Environment 360. Reprinted by permission.

from industry to make the large investment necessary to stanch the leaks.

Last month, the Obama administration announced a plan to reduce methane emissions from a host of sources, including landfills, cattle, and the oil and gas industry. The U.S. Environmental Protection Agency (EPA) has pledged to identify approaches to cut so-called "fugitive" methane emissions from oil and gas drilling by this fall and to issue new rules by 2016 as President Obama's term in office comes to an end. Roughly nine percent of U.S. greenhouse gas emissions come from methane.

"The strategy is a good plan of action," said Vignesh Gowrishankar, a staff scientist at Natural Resources Defense Council. "But more needs to be done. The most important thing is to ensure that EPA implements stronger standards that go after methane directly and include existing equipment in the field because that is what is leaking."

Colorado, a major oil and gas producer, in February became the first state to impose regulations requiring producers to find and fix methane leaks. And as public concerns mount over the environmental fallout from the fracking boom, even states such as Texas are examining whether to adopt tighter methane regulations.

Industry has lived with methane leaks, despite the value of capturing and eventually selling the methane, because of the expense involved in stopping fugitive emissions. Fixing the problem would require a comprehensive approach that would involve not only detecting methane leaks, but also instituting a host of engineering and mechanical fixes along the entire chain of production and processing, from the wellhead to pipes.

Reducing fugitive methane emissions can be classified into easy fixes, such as tightening pipe flanges, to harder ones such as replacing valves in compressor stations that constantly pump gas under intense pressure, said Bryan Willson, program director at the U.S. Department of Energy's Advanced Research Projects Agency-Energy (ARPA-E).

There is less incentive for the industry—particularly smaller, cash-constrained companies—to make fixes that require more personnel, time, and money, yielding a lower return-on-investment. Some of the fixes, such as "vapor recovery units" that prevent gas from volatilizing from storage tanks, come with a price tag of $100,000 each, said Gowrishankar. One study found storage tanks to be a significant source of volatile organic compounds and methane emissions in Texas' Barnett Shale region.

A key question is whether the U.S. can achieve a significant reduction in methane emissions as the fracking boom continues to expand and older equipment becomes more prone to problems. With close to 500,000 hydraulically fractured gas wells alone and hundreds of thousands of miles of pipelines, just figuring out the scope of the problem, let alone fixing all the leaks, is a daunting challenge, experts say.

Calculating exactly how much methane is escaping during the fracking and processing of oil and gas is exceedingly difficult. Estimates of methane emissions range from 1.5 percent to 9 percent. Getting a clearer sense of the scope of the problem is vital; although methane only lingers in the atmosphere for 10 to 20 years—as opposed to hundreds of years for carbon dioxide—recent studies show that methane is 34 times as potent a greenhouse gas as CO_2. Failing to stop widespread methane leaks from the global oil and gas industry in the coming decades could significantly exacerbate global warming, many experts say.

With an expected 56-percent increase over the next 25 years in U.S. natural gas production alone—most of which is expected to come from fracking—the problem of methane leaks is going to get worse "unless we make the investment" in lower-emissions technology, said Michael Obeiter, a senior associate in the climate and energy program at the World Resources Institute.

In February, Brandt and 15 co-authors published a paper in *Science*, based on a review of more than 200 previous studies, concluding that leaks of methane from drilling sites were 50 percent higher than previously estimated by the EPA. "A variety of evidence" points to emissions higher than 1.5 percent, Brandt said.

Environmental groups such as the World Resources Institute, Environmental Defense Fund, and the Natural Resources Defense Council say a mix of regulation and new technology in detection and emission-control engineering could push the industry to address the problem of leaks.

Methane emissions from oil and gas drilling are broken down into two different problem areas. The first is outdated equipment that emits much more methane than newer, low-emissions technology. The second is a string of leaks in the system, many which can be difficult to detect. "If we can develop a way to find these leaks cheaply, frequently, and in an automated fashion," most of the leaks can be detected and fixed, said Brandt.

Obeiter lists two major equipment upgrades that have already shown promise in the field, but have not been widely adopted by industry.

The first is the use of plunger lift systems at new and existing wells during "liquids unloading," which are operations that clear water and other liquids from the system. The second is replacing existing high-bleed pneumatic devices with low-bleed equivalents throughout natural gas systems.

Some companies such as Encana—a natural gas producer that has 4,000 gas wells in Colorado—are retrofitting outdated equipment prone to leaking, and installing technology to capture leaks at the wellhead. The company began replacing existing high-bleed pneumatic devices before the conversion was mandated in Colorado's new regulations, said Doug Hock, a spokesman for the company. Hock calls the new rules in Colorado "tough but reasonable" and says they provide the industry in the state with regulatory certainty going forward.

But even if every state mirrored Colorado and every oil and gas company took steps such as Encana is taking, a significant amount of methane would still be leaking—and much of it undetected, says Mark Zondlo, a professor of engineering at Princeton University.

That's because many methane leaks are caused by more erratic and episodic factors, such as a valve or storage-tank hatch suddenly stuck open. Hence the need for "continuous measurements" for methane leaks across large areas, Zondlo said.

Currently, there is a lot of "guessing" on the part of the industry and researchers as to where and how frequently the majority of leaks are happening, says Zondlo.

Industry representatives say the methane leakage rate is at the low end of estimates, about 1.5 percent, placing industry second behind emissions attributed to livestock, said Katie Brown, spokesperson for Energy in Depth, a program of the Independent Petroleum Association of America.

To achieve climate benefits from natural gas, environmental groups estimate the leakage rate during gas drilling must remain below 1 percent. "Cutting methane leakage rates from natural gas systems to less than 1 percent of total production would ensure that the climate impacts of natural gas are lower than coal or diesel fuel over any time horizon," Obeiter said.

But Sandra Steingraber, an environmentalist and scholar in residence at Ithaca College, compares chasing methane leaks and retrofitting old equipment to "putting filters on cigarettes." She said that even reducing methane leaks by 30 to 40 percent will be too little too late to help slow climate change, especially as the industry expands.

Currently, many companies are using methane-leak detection tools, such as infrared cameras, that are too labor-intensive and fail to find many leaks. What's needed, say Obeiter and other experts, is an industry-wide method for monitoring and repairing methane leaks across the production and processing system.

Zondlo recently developed a methane sensor mounted on a remote—controlled aircraft built at the University of Texas at Dallas. In October, the aircraft was used to quantify emission rates from well pads and a compressor station in the Barnett Shale region. Zondlo has been partnering with other groups that fly drones over fracking areas to detect leaks.

Robert B. Jackson, an ecologist and energy expert at Duke University, also has been testing drones to detect fugitive methane emissions. The main drawback, he says, is the payload. "Carrying a big camera or methane sensor, a drone might be able to stay in the air for 30 minutes," says Jackson. "It's difficult to screen a shale play with that kind of time."

Engineers are trying to develop lighter sensors that will allow drones to stay in the air longer. "I'm very bullish long-term on using drones to measure leaks," Jackson said. "Are we there yet right now? No."

In the Pinedale Anticline natural gas field in Wyoming, Shane Murphy and Robert Field of the University of Wyoming recently outfitted a Mercedes Sprinter van with a mass spectrometer and other high-powered scientific instruments to measure volatile organic compounds and methane. When combined with meteorological instrumentation and sophisticated software, these technologies can detect methane plumes and quantify emission rates from specific sources—all from inside the van. The equipment records readings every half-second, which allows it to be used on the move. "This approach can cover a lot of ground," Field said.

Study Shows Methane Emission from Fracking Is Low

Steve Everley

Steve Everley is a Managing Director in the Strategic Communications practice at FTI Consulting and is based in Dallas. He is a member of the Energy & Natural Resources sector.

Methane emissions from natural gas production—including hydraulic fracturing, or "fracking"—are lower than previously thought, according to a major new study from researchers at the University of Texas. The research was done in close coordination with the Environmental Defense Fund (EDF), a major U.S. environmental organization.

The study, published today in two parts in the journal *Environmental Science & Technology*, finds that methane emissions from the upstream portion of the supply chain are only 0.38 percent of production. That's about 10 percent lower than what the same research team found in a study released in September 2013. The researchers also noted that a small number of sites accounted for the majority of emissions, suggesting that technologies already in use across the industry are effectively managing methane leakage.

The emissions rate in the study released today also corresponds with the U.S. EPA's estimates for methane emissions, which are far lower than what anti-fracking groups frequently claim are "leaking" as a result of fracking. Earlier this year, EPA observed that methane emissions from fracking have fallen by 73 percent since just 2011. Since 1990, methane emissions from U.S. natural gas systems have declined by nearly 17 percent.

The UT/EDF study found pneumatic controllers (onsite devices that use gas pressure to control valves and other equipment) have emissions that are slightly higher than what's reported by EPA (the

"New Study Finds Decrease in Methane Emissions from Fracking," by Steve Everley, Energy In Depth, December 9, 2014. energyindepth.org. Reprinted by permission.

study suggests these emissions are about 17 percent higher than what EPA estimated). But emissions from liquids unloading—the process of removing liquids from the well bore—were slightly lower than EPA's estimates. The authors noted that their data "represent the most extensive set of measurements of emissions from liquid unloadings in the scientific literature."

The overall picture shows methane emissions are slightly lower than previously thought, according to the study:

> The overall average emission rates reported in this work are lower than the previous data sets reported by Allen, et al. for the United States, and for British Columbia and Alberta.

A chart accompanying the research shows total methane emissions of 2,185 gigagrams (Gg), or approximately 0.38 percent of total natural gas withdrawals and production in 2012, according to data from the U.S. Energy Information Administration.

Last week, Energy in Depth released a report showing declines in methane emissions in many shale basins across the country, including the Permian Basin and Eagle Ford region in Texas; major producing areas in Oklahoma; and in the Marcellus and Utica shale regions in Ohio and Pennsylvania.

Confirms Previous Studies

The UT/EDF study is only the latest in a long line of existing research and peer-reviewed papers that confirm the environmental advantages of natural gas. A brief list is below:

- National Renewable Energy Laboratory: "On a per-unit electrical output basis, harmonization reveals that median estimates of GHG emissions from shale gas-generated electricity are similar to those for conventional natural gas, with both approximately half that of the central tendency of coal."
- U.N. IPCC: "A key development since AR4 is the rapid deployment of hydraulic fracturing and horizontal drilling technologies, which has increased and diversified the gas

supply… this is an important reason for a reduction of GHG emissions in the United States."

- Cornell Univ.: "Using more reasonable leakage rates and bases of comparison, shale gas has a GHG footprint that is half and perhaps a third that of coal."
- Univ. of Maryland: "GHG impacts of shale gas are…only 56%that of coal…. rguments that shale gas is more polluting than coal are largely unjustified."
- Carnegie Mellon Univ.: "Natural gas from the Marcellus shale has generally lower life cycle GHG emissions than coal for production of electricity in the absence of any effective carbon capture and storage processes, by 20-50% depending upon plant efficiencies and natural gas emissions variability." NOTE: Study partially funded by the Sierra Club
- Massachusetts Institute of Technology: "Although fugitive emissions from the overall natural gas sector are a proper concern, it is incorrect to suggest that shale gas-related hydraulic fracturing has substantially altered the overall GHG intensityof natural gas production."
- NOTE: Coauthor is a lead author of the IPCC's Fifth Assessment Report
- National Energy Technology Laboratory (U.S. DOE): "Natural gas-fired baseload power production has life cycle greenhouse gas emissions 42 to 53 percent lower than those for coal-fired baseload electricity, after accounting for a wide range of variability and compared across different assumptions of climate impact timing."
- Joint Institute for Strategic Energy Analysis/NREL: "Based on analysis of more than 16,000 sources of air-pollutant emissions reported in a state inventory of upstream and midstream natural gas industry, life cycle greenhouse gas emissions associated with electricity generated from Barnett Shale gas extracted in 2009 were found to be very similar to conventional natural gas and less than half thoseof coal-fired electricity generation."

- AEA Technology (for the European Commission): "In our analysis, emissions from shale gas generation are significantly lower (41% to 49%) than emissions from electricity generated from coal. This is on the basis of methane having a 100 year GWP of 25. This finding is consistent [with] most other studies into the GHG emissions arising from shale gas."
- Worldwatch Institute: "[W]e conclude that on average, U.S. natural gas-fired electricity generation still emitted 47 percent less GHGsthan coal from source to use using the IPCC's 100-year global warming potential for methane of 25."
- The Breakthrough Institute: "The climate benefits of natural gas are real and are significant. Recent lifecycle assessments studies confirm that natural gas has just half as much global warming potentialas coal."

The head of the U.S. EPA has also said, "Responsible development of natural gas is an important part of our work to curb climate change."

A Rebuke to Anti-Fracking Advocacy

The findings from the UT/EDF study cast more doubt upon the claims of groups that oppose fracking, who have made "methane leaks" a key component of their advocacy against U.S. oil and natural gas development.

Last year, *Gasland* filmmaker Josh Fox wrote that President Obama "does not have the right information on fracked gas," alleging that "methane is leaking like crazy" from oil and natural gas production activities. Food & Water Watch, one of the most aggressive anti-fracking groups in the country, claimed last month that natural gas is "proving to be more of a 'gangplank' to climate chaos," based upon claims of high methane leakage rates. The group linked to a 2013 op-ed by Cornell University activist Tony Ingraffea, whose claims were refuted by climate scientists just days after his column was published.

Al Gore has also criticized fracking, based upon assumptions of high methane emissions.

Most scientists, however, have found that natural gas will retain its environmental and climate advantages if methane emissions are kept under two to three percent of total production. The U.S. EPA's data, which are largely corroborated by today's UT/EDF study, suggest a leakage rate of only about 1.5 percent.

Methane a Fixable Problem

Although the research does show methane emissions on the right trajectory, the study also finds that a "small subset of natural gas wells are responsible for the majority of methane emissions," according to the press release associated with the report. That means most wells and their associated equipment have been effectively designed to mitigate or even eliminate emissions.

As the authors noted regarding pneumatic controllers:

> ...the measurements reported in this work had large numbers of devices for which no emissions were detected during the sampling period (p. 14; emphasis added).

The finding that a "small subset" of sites is responsible for most emissions meshes with what EDF President Fred Krupp said earlier this year, when he noted that "we have the technology" to reduce methane emissions. "This is essentially a data acquisition and management problem—the kind that we know we can solve," Krupp wrote in an op-ed for the *New York Times*, co-authored by Michael Bloomberg.

The UT study was funded in part by EDF and several energy companies who agreed to participate in the research, and who provided access to the well sites for direct measurements. According to the study, the sites where measurements occurred were not selected by the companies, but rather chosen at random by the researchers themselves.

Sierra Club Credits Natural Gas for Reducing Carbon Emissions

Seth Whitehead

Seth Whitehead is a spokesman for Energy In Depth, *an education and research program sponsored by the Independent Petroleum Association of America.*

The Sierra Club released a report last week attempting to argue that its "Beyond Coal" campaign is the reason that the United States has been able to achieve dramatic greenhouse gas reductions even though every credible organization from the Intergovernmental Panel on Climate Change (IPCC) to the International Energy Agency (IEA) to the Energy Information Administration (EIA) has said that it's thanks to fracking and the increased use of natural gas that U.S. CO_2 emissions are at a 27 year low.

Of course, this is the same organization responsible for the "Beyond Natural Gas" campaign, which seeks to end the use of natural gas—the very fuel that is providing these dramatic declines in emissions. So it's no surprise Sierra Club trumpeted tweet by Bloomberg Philanthropies, one of its partners in the "Beyond Coal" campaign [showing a forecasted drop in carbon pollution in the U.S.].

But while the Sierra Club attempts to take all the credit, even this organization can't really get away without (reluctantly) acknowledging that natural gas has played a huge role in reducing carbon emissions:

> We project that as a result of recent coal retirements, as well as advocacy for related policy measures like efficiency and demand response and market forces including historically low natural

"Sierra Club (Reluctantly) Admits Fracking has Helped Lower CO2 Emissions," by Seth Whitehead, Energy In Depth, November 9, 2015. Reprinted by permission.

> gas prices, electric sector coal use in 2015 will be approximately 9 percent lower than in 2014…

Interestingly, Sierra Club's own research indicates a future outlook spearheaded by natural gas is even brighter. In a hypothetical scenario set forth in the report in which all U.S. coal-burning power plants set to retire in the next 10 years were replaced exclusively with natural gas rather than with renewables, the Sierra Club projects CO_2 emissions would continue to plummet.

> … we analyzed the carbon emission impacts of replacing one half of the U.S. coal fleet by 2025, under two replacement scenarios: 100 percent zero-carbon clean energy and 100 percent natural gas… we could accelerate EPA's 2030 CPP target by as much as 5 years depending on whether we replace coal plants likely to retire in the coming years with zero-carbon renewable energy or natural gas.

A 100 percent renewable scenario would drive emissions even lower, according to the Sierra Club, but such a scenario is not realistic. The Energy Information Administration (EIA) estimates that by 2040, 80 percent of our energy will still be fossil-fuel based. In addition, renewables will need natural gas in order for them to grow into a more significant part of our energy mix.

The graphic also clearly indicates the natural-gas only scenario would actually reduce carbon emissions below the Clean Power Plan projections (which include a mix of renewables and natural gas) at one point in the early 2020s. And over the 15-year timeframe shown, emission drops would be right in line with Clean Power Plan.

So let's get this straight: The Sierra Club opposes a technology that its own research shows will help address its No. 1 environmental concern—global warming—by reducing carbon emissions.

Maybe that's why—in an attempt to save face—the organization has been forced to take the delusional stance that its "Beyond Coal" campaign is solely responsible for coal plant retirements heading into December's climate change conference in Paris:

> As a result of our work, buoyed by plummeting clean energy prices, we have secured record coal retirements over the past five years, catapulting the U.S. into a leadership role in transitioning our economy to lower-carbon sources of energy.

Of course, Sierra Club's self-serving conclusion is all premised on the false notion that power plant conversion to renewables in the past five years has played a larger role in reducing CO_2 emissions than conversion to natural gas.

But the facts suggest otherwise.

So far in 2015 (through August), coal has accounted for 35 percent of electrical generation (down 10 percent from 2010), while natural gas has accounted for 32 percent (up 8 percent from 2010) and renewables 13 percent (up 3 percent from 2010).

In terms of thousand kilowatt hours over the last 12 months in which data is available (August 2014 to August 2015), coal is down 405 thousand kwh since 2010, while natural gas has increased 279 thousand kwh and renewables are up 108 thousand kwh. According to the Sierra Club's report, 41,978 megawatts of coal-fired electricity have been retired since 2010, and 15,760 megawatts of coal-generated electricity have already been retired in 2015, with potentially 6,978 mw projected to go offline by the end of the year. Renewables have filled just three percent of the void.

So any way you slice it—considering natural gas produces half of the carbon emissions of coal when it burns—shale gas has played a huge role in reducing carbon emissions from the power sector.

In fairness, giving credit where credit is due is simply not in the best interest of the Sierra Club, which once supported natural gas as the bridge fuel before abruptly doing a 180-degree turn in 2013, declaring its disdain for natural gas in a move that many have speculated had more to do with political expediency than logic.

Meanwhile the EIA has said natural gas has prevented more than one billion metric tons of carbon dioxide from being emitted from the nation's power plants since 2005. The IPCC, which the Sierra Club has called the "gold standard" for climate science has said "the rapid deployment of hydraulic fracturing and horizontal drilling technologies, which has increased and diversified the gas supply… is an important reason for a reduction of GHG emissions in the United States."

A report released this week by the Manhattan Institute shows that natural gas is responsible for nearly 20 percent of carbon dioxide emission cuts since 2007 and that for every ton of CO_2 emission reductions attributable to solar power, 13 tons can be attributed to natural gas. That is because natural gas is quickly becoming the electrical generation fuel of choice, as it became the leading source of U.S. electricity for the first time in April 2015. Not coincidently, monthly power plant emissions reached 27-year low in April that month.

In other words, evidence of shale gas' massive role in reducing U.S. power sector carbon emissions to nearly 10 percent below 2000 levels has become so overwhelming that even the Sierra Club can't deny natural gas' climate benefits any longer.

People Near Fracking Sites See Increased Risk of Health Problems

National Resource Defense Council

The National Resource Defense Council makes it its mission to safeguard the planet, including the people, plants, animals, and natural systems on which all life on Earth depends.

A growing body of evidence shows that people both near and far from oil and gas drilling are exposed to fracking-related air pollution that can cause at least five major types of health impacts, according to a new comprehensive analysis of scientific studies to-date by the Natural Resources Defense Council. The health impacts include respiratory problems, birth defects, blood disorders, cancer and nervous system impacts, raising serious concerns for workers and people living closest to wells, as well as entire regions with high volumes of oil and gas activity.

"The health risks from fracking are not limited to what's in our drinking water—oil and gas operations are also poisoning the air we breathe," said NRDC senior scientist Miriam Rotkin-Ellman. "While industry continues to try to sweep the impacts of fracking under a rug, the science keeps revealing serious health threats—for workers, families living nearby and entire regions with heavy oil and gas activity."

Fracking Fumes: Air Pollution from Hydraulic Fracturing Threatens Public Health and Communities provides the most comprehensive analysis of available science to-date on toxic air pollution from oil and gas development. It identifies an emerging pattern in the science revealing unsafe levels of air pollution near fracking sites around the country. More research is needed to better understand a wide range of other threats that have emerged.

"REPORT: Five Major Health Threats from Fracking-Related Air Pollution," Natural Resources Defense Council, December 16, 2014. Reprinted with permission from the Natural Resources Defense Council.

The report breaks down the health impacts that scientists have identified on the local, regional and global scales. It shows that health threats from air pollution are not limited to communities with drilling directly in their backyards. Rather, entire regions with high levels of oil and gas activity are paying the price with smog-filled skies and respiratory problems.

Global

In addition to carbon pollution, fracking operations emit massive amounts of methane pollution, which drive global climate change. Methane warms the climate at least 80 times more than an equal amount of carbon dioxide over a 20-year period.

Regional

Nitrogen oxides and volatile organic compounds (VOCs) form ground-level ozone. In communities where there is a lot of drilling, this can cause respiratory and cardiovascular effects on a regional scale, even for those who don't live in close proximity to wells. Impacts include coughs, shortness of breath, airway and lung inflammation, decreased lung function, worsening of asthma and other respiratory diseases, cardiac arrhythmia, increased risk of heart disease, heart attacks, stroke, increased hospital admissions and premature mortality.

Local

Those living or working closest to wells are at the highest risk. In addition to the aforementioned health threats, they can also be exposed to diesel particulate matter and other toxics, including carcinogens. As a result, they are also at risk for eye, nose and throat irritation, brain and nervous system problems including headaches, lightheadedness and disorientation, blood and bone marrow damage leading to anemia and immunological problems, reproductive system effects, birth defects and harm to the developing fetus, and cancer.

Of these impacts, there is the greatest amount of evidence raising concern about risks for the following health impacts:

Respiratory Problems

Impacts can include asthma attacks, shortness of breath, difficulty breathing and lung disease. Levels of pollutants high enough to cause respiratory problems, particularly for vulnerable populations such as children, have been found both close to fracking sites and in regions with intense oil and gas activity. Workers have been found to be at risk of permanent lung damage caused by exposure to silica fracking sand.

Nervous System Impacts

Exposure to these pollutants, such as VOCs and hydrogen sulfide, can cause neurological problems ranging from dizziness and headaches to seizures and loss of consciousness. Multiple studies have measured benzene levels close to fracking sites that are higher than the thresholds set to protect people from these impacts.

Birth Defects & Harm to the Developing Fetus

A number of VOCs and polycyclic aromatic hydrocarbons (PAHs) have been found to interfere with fetal and child development resulting in harm to the developing heart, brain and nervous system. Because even short-term exposures to these pollutants at critical moments of development can result in long-lasting harm, health experts have identified this as a threat for communities living in close proximity to fracking sites.

Blood Disorders

The levels of benzene measured in multiple studies were high enough to raise concerns about permanent damage to blood-forming organs, resulting in harm to bone marrow and anemia, if there were repeated or chronic exposures.

Cancer

Cancer-causing pollutants like benzene, formaldehyde, diesel particulates and PAHs, have also been found in the air near fracking sites. Repeated or chronic exposures to these pollutants can cause an increased risk of cancer.

Studies have also found pollutants linked to other health impacts near fracking operations, including heart problems and harm to the liver, kidney, endocrine, immune, reproductive, gastrointestinal and auditory systems. More research is needed to better understand the level of risk for these impacts to workers, neighboring families and communities.

Unfortunately, air pollution impacts have gone largely ignored by federal and state agencies to date. The Environmental Protection Agency, as well as state governments, must address air pollution from oil and gas development in order to protect the health of neighboring residents.

With approximately one in four Americans now living within a mile of an oil or gas well, and fracking spreading the industry's reach even further across the country, this report underscores the need for immediate action to protect public health.

Fracking Pollutes the Air

Jesse Coleman

Jesse Coleman is a researcher with the Greenpeace Investigations team. His focus is on front groups, fracking, and the oil and gas industry. Jesse's work has been featured in The Guardian, The New York Times, The Colbert Report, Al-Jazeera, MSNBC, and NPR.

With approval from major drilling and fracking companies, Colorado Governor John Hickenlooper has proposed a set of regulations to reduce pollution from methane and other dangerous gases leaked by the oil and gas industry. The rules are focused on fracking wells, a mostly unregulated drilling technology that has allowed an unprecedented increase in fossil fuel extraction in Colorado and across the nation. The proposed regulations address a serious hazard posed by the massive growth of fracking in Colorado. There are over 51,000 fracking wells in Colorado, most of which have been drilled in the last four years. These wells, which produce both gas and oil, also leak gases like methane, the primary component of natural gas and a potent greenhouse gas. Methane is up to 105 times as powerful as carbon dioxide as a greenhouse pollutant. Scientists have theorized that fugitive emissions of methane from fracking wells could make gas worse than coal pollution for the climate.

Fracking wells also leak volatile organic compounds (VOCs), which cause asthma, cancer, and severe illness. Oil and gas emissions are the main source of volatile organic compounds in Colorado and the third-largest source of nitrogen oxides. There have been many reported cases of illness from fracking pollution in Colorado since the boom began, causing families to uproot for the sake of the health of their children.

Smog caused by fracking emissions have already sent toxic ozone readings soaring in what was once pristine Rocky Mountain habitat. Ozone-forming air pollution measured along the Colorado Front Range by scientists is up to twice the amount that government regulators have calculated should exist. The researchers pinpoint oil and gas development as the main source. Studies of fugitive methane emissions from fracking have found astounding levels of pollution. A study form the Uinta basin in Utah, found massive methane leaks from fracking wells. In Uinta, wells were estimated to be leaking 60 tons of methane per hour. The response from fracking groups to the new rules has been tepid.The Environmental Defense Fund (EDF), a group which claims fracking can be done safely, helped create the proposed legislation. Fracking has grown increasingly controversial as people in shale areas feel the environmental and health impacts of the hundreds of thousands of wells drilled each year. In the debate over fracking, EDF has played the role of the pro-industry environmental group. They have partnered with the oil industry to produce a series of studies on the dangers of methane pollution from fracking. Their first study, which was published in September of 2013, found surprisingly low methane pollution from specific parts of the fracking process. However, the sampling of fracking wells used in the study was controlled by the gas corporations who owned them, and many of those involved in the study were later found to have significant ties to the gas industry. EDF is involved in a congruent partnership with the industry called the Center for Sustainable Shale Development (CSSD). As part of this group, which includes Shell, Chevron and other major gas industry players, EDF would give fracking wells an environmental seal of approval, in the form of a CSSD Certification. The biggest fracking lobbyist groups, who generally oppose all regulation of the industry, do not support the new rules. A spokeswoman for the American Petroleum Institute said the group hadn't taken a position on the proposed regulations. Colorado Petroleum Association president Stan Dempsey questioned the state's authority and the need for new rules.

As the fracking industry tacitly admits by supporting this regulation, fracking poses a serious and as yet unmitigated danger to air quality. It is unknown when these regulations would take effect and given the number of wells already drilled in Colorado and the cost associated with retrofitting all of them, it is unclear if old wells will be required to adhere to the new rules. Air and water pollution from fracking is already impacting people throughout the United States, and if air quality is in danger from fracking in Colorado, it is in danger wherever fracking is occurring.

Fracking Will Not Reduce Net Greenhouse Gas Emission

Alex Kirby

Alex Kirby is a former BBC journalist and environment correspondent. He now works with universities, charities and international agencies to improve their media skills, and with developing world journalists keen to specialize in environmental reporting.

As advanced technology triggers the boom in extraction of natural gas, a new study warns that market forces mean the cheaper fossil fuel could replace not just coal, but also low-emission renewable and nuclear energy. LONDON, 15 October 2014 – The argument that fracking can help to reduce greenhouse gas emissions is misguided, according to an international scientific study, because the amount of extra fossil fuel it will produce will cancel out the benefits of its lower pollution content. The study, published today in the journal *Nature*, recognises that technologies such as fracking have triggered a boom in natural gas. But the authors say this will not lead to a reduction of overall greenhouse gas emissions. Although natural gas produces only half the CO_2 emissions of coal for each unit of energy, its growing availability will make it cheaper, they say, so it will add to total energy supply and only partly replace coal.

Advantage nullified

Their study, based on what they say is "an unprecedented international comparison of computer simulations", shows that this market effect nullifies the advantage offered by the lower pollution content of the gas. The lead author, Haewon McJeon, staff scientist at the Joint Global Change Research Institute, a

"Scientists refute lower emissions claim for fracking," by Alex Kirby, Climate News Network, October 15, 2014. http://climatenewsnetwork.net/scientists-refute-lower-emissions-claim-for-fracking/.

partnership between the US Department of Energy's Pacific Northwest National Laboratory (PNNL) and the University of Maryland, said: "The upshot is that abundant natural gas alone will not rescue us from climate change." Fracking, horizontal drilling and other techniques have led to surging gas production, especially in the US. "Global deployment of advanced technology could double or triple global natural gas production by 2050," McJeon said. This might eventually mean not lower CO_2 emissions, but emissions by the middle of the century up to 10% higher than they would otherwise be. The report, which is the work of five research groups from Germany, the US, Austria, Italy and Australia, said the replacement of coal by natural gas was fairly limited. And it might replace not just coal, the study had found, but low-emission renewable energy and nuclear power as well. One of the co-authors, Nico Bauer, a sustainable solutions expert at the Potsdam Institute for Climate Impact Research (PIK), Germany, said : "The high hopes that natural gas will help reduce global warming because of technical superiority to coal turn out to be misguided because market effects are dominating. "The main factor here is that an abundance of natural gas leads to a price drop and expansion of total primary energy supply." Not only could this lead to an overall increase in energy consumption and in emissions, but increased gas production would mean higher emissions of methane from drilling leakages and pipelines. The research groups projected what the world might be like in 2050, both with and without a natural gas boom. They used five different computer models, which included not just energy use and production, but also the broader economy and the climate system.

"When we first saw little change in greenhouse gas emissions in our model, we thought we had made a mistake, because we were fully expecting to see a significant reduction in emissions," said James Edmonds, chief scientist at the Joint Global Change Research Institute. "But when we saw all five teams reporting little difference in climate change, we knew we were on to something." Ottmar Edenhofer, chief economist of PIK and co-chair of the

Intergovernmental Panel on Climate Change (IPCC) working group on mitigation, said: "The findings show that effective climate stabilisation can be achieved only through emissions pricing. "This requires international political co-operation and binding agreements. Technological advances can reduce the costs of climate policies, but they cannot replace policies."

Article of faith

The widespread use of shale gas continues to attract policymakers, and for some it is almost an article of faith. It recently received the IPCC's endorsement, with Professor Edenhofer himself apparently backing it. In the UK, a senior Conservative politician, Owen Paterson, is urging more fracking to increase Britain's shale gas supplies. Paterson, who lost his job as Environment Secretary in July, today gave the annual lecture to the climate-sceptic Global Warming Policy Foundation, arguing against wind power and for "investment in four possible common sense policies: shale gas, combined heat and power, small modular nuclear reactors, and demand management." Paterson also said that the UK should suspend or scrap its Climate Change Act, which commits it to cutting CO_2 emissions by more than 80% on 1990 levels by 2050, unless other countries follow suit. His former Cabinet colleague, the Energy and Climate Change Secretary, Ed Davey, said that scrapping the legislation would be "one of the most stupid economic decisions imaginable."

Chapter 3

Does Fracking Endanger Our Water Supply?

Overview: There Is Conflict About Fracking's Impact on the Water Supply

Greenpeace

Greenpeace is the leading independent campaigning organization that uses peaceful protest and creative communication to expose global environmental problems and to promote solutions that are essential to a green and peaceful future.

In order to frack, an enormous amount of water is mixed with various toxic chemical compounds to create frack fluid. This frack fluid is further contaminated by the heavy metals and radioactive elements that exist naturally in the shale. A significant portion of the frack fluid returns to the surface, where it can spill or be dumped into rivers and streams. Underground water supplies can also be contaminated by fracking, through migration of gas and frack fluid underground.

Water Use

In order to hydraulically fracture shale and extract the hydrocarbons, large quantities of water and chemicals must be injected underground. Thus fracking can pose a threat to local water resources, especially in areas where water is already scarce like the Barnett shale in Texas. In the Marcellus Shale region, the most expansive shale play in the United States, 2 to 10 million gallons of water are needed every time a well is fractured. Because wells can be fractured multiple times, the total amount of water used for fracking is unknown and can vary by location and technology. In western states like Texas and Colorado, over 3.6 million gallons are needed per fracture. In 2010, the U.S. EPA estimated that 70 to 140 billion gallons of water were used to fracture just 35,000 wells in the United States, more than was used by the city of Denver, Colorado in the same time period. As of 2012, the fracking industry

"Fracking's Environmental Impacts: Water," Greenpeace. Reprinted by permission.

has drilled around 1.2 million wells, and is slated to add at least 35,000 new wells every year. (Jeff Goodell, "The Big Fracking Bubble: The Scam Behind the Gas Boom," Rolling Stone 3/12/12)

Because of the cost to truck water in from further away, companies prefer to use water from sources as close to the well as possible, which can result in significant impacts on local waterways and overburden local water treatment facilities. In Texas, which is suffering dangerous drought conditions, fracking continues even as water use by citizens is restricted, the landscape wilts and the animal life dies. In 2011 the Wall Street Journal reported that the diversion of water for fracking oil and gas wells is also a serious threat to ranchers and other businesses in Texas. (Russell Gold and Ana Campoy, "Oil's Growing Thirst for Water," *Wall Street Journal*, 12/6/2011)

Storage Impacts

Because of the tremendous amount of water needed for hydraulic fracturing, fresh water must be acquired, transported, and stored for every well pad. To manage the massive amounts of water necessary for the hydraulic fracturing process, drillers build large open air pits called impoundments next to the well pads, to store the water before it is used and after it returns to the surface.

There are two types of impoundments, those that hold drilling waste, used while drilling the well bore, and impoundments for the fracking fluid. The frack fluid pits are larger and contain toxic fracking fluid. These open pits have been linked to animal deaths and health effects in humans.

In Texas, which has few laws regarding wastewater disposal, there is no requirement to line the pits to prevent seepage.

Fracking Fluids: A Toxic Brew

During the hydraulic fracturing of a well, water is mixed with various chemicals to make a toxic brew called frack fluid. Until recently, neither the federal nor state governments required drilling companies to disclose the ingredients used in frack fluids. Some states have begun to require that companies disclose the chemicals they use, but even in such cases, companies can withhold some chemical names under trade secret exemptions. As a result, a comprehensive list of chemicals used in the fracking process does not exist. Some states have begun to require that companies disclose the chemicals they use, but even in such cases, confidential business information claims result in only partial disclosures. Corporations involved in fracking, like ExxonMobil, have inserted loopholes in drilling legislation that allow them to keep various chemicals used in the fracking process secret.

Some companies have disclosed the contents of their frack fluid in response to community concerns and congressional pressure. In April 2011, an industry group known as the Interstate Oil and Gas Compact Commission launched www.fracfocus.org, a web-based disclosure database for wells drilled after 2010. In addition, a Congressional investigation found that between 2005 and 2009 oil and gas service companies used 29 different chemicals in their fracking fluid known to cause cancer or other health risks. (House Energy and Commerce Committee, "Chemicals Used in Hydraulic Fracturing," April, 2011)

Gas companies routinely claim that frack fluid is harmless because the concentration of chemical additives is low, about two percent. But just 2% of the billions of gallons of frack fluid created by gas drillers measures up to the use of hundreds of tons of toxic chemicals. A 2011 report to Congress estimated that from 2005 to 2009, 14 leading fracking companies used (before mixing with water) 780 million gallons of 750 different chemicals. (House Energy and Commerce Committee, Minority Staff Report, "Chemicals Used in Hydraulic Fracturing," April, 2011)

Drilling wastewater is so poisonous, when a gas company that legally doused a patch of West Virginia forest with salty wastewater from a drilling operation, it killed ground vegetation within days and more than half the trees within two years. Wastewater from fracking has also been linked to livestock and family pet deaths across the country.

Moreover, many chemicals used in fracking have been documented to have deleterious health effects at small levels of exposure.

Some of the chemicals that comprise frack fluid are highly toxic and cancer causing, like Benzene, Toluene, 2-butoxyethanol (a main ingredient to anti-freeze and oil dispersants), and heavy metals. The Endocrine Disruptor Exchange (TEDX) identified 353 chemicals used in fracking, many of which can cause cancer and other serious health, even in small doses.

Once the frack fluid mixture is injected into the ground it can also pick up or entrain further contaminants, like radium, a cancer-causing radioactive particle found deep within the Marcellus and other shales. Radium has a half life of over 1,000 years and is produced from Uranium, which has a much longer half life. Because Radium is water soluble, all frack fluid used in the Marcellus Shale becomes radioactive to some degree.

Contamination of Water Wells and Gas Migration

One of the gravest threats posed by fracking is the contamination of drinking water wells, vital sources of water for many rural communities. Though the industry has attempted to obscure evidence of well water contamination by fracking, multiple instances have come to light.

- In Pennsylvania, Colorado, Ohio and Wyoming, fracking has been linked to drinking water contamination and property damage. (See Propublica's series of reports on fracking)
- A Duke study examining 60 sites in New York and Pennsylvania found "systematic evidence for methane contamination" in household drinking water. Water wells half a mile from drilling operations were contaminated by methane at 17 times the rate of those farther from gas developments. Although methane in water has not been studied closely as a health hazard, it can seep into houses and build up to explosive levels.

- In December 2011, US EPA released a 121-page draft report linking the contamination of drinking water wells near the town of Pavillion, Wyoming to nearby gas drilling.
- An investigation by ProPublica found that years after their wells were contaminated by nearby fracking operations, EPA began to supply water to residents of Dimock, Pennsylvania.
- In New York, claims have already been filed against the Anschutz Exploration Corporation and its subcontractors on behalf of nine families for the contamination of their drinking waterdue to natural gas exploration and drilling.
- A scene in *Gasland*, a documentary in which a homeowner was able to light the water flowing out of his kitchen tap, made many people aware of the dangers of fracking. Scientific American also published a ProPublica investigation that found "a string of documented cases of gas escaping into drinking water—in Pennsylvania and other states."
- A 1987 report concluded that hydraulic fracturing fluids or gel used by the Kaiser Exploration and Mining Company contaminated a well roughly 600 feet away on the property of James Parsons in Jackson County, W.Va.

In spite of the evidence, the oil and gas industry routinely claims that fracking has never resulted in water contamination.

How Fracking Contaminates

Groundwater becomes contaminated by hydraulic fracturing in a number of ways, including leakage from liquid storage areas, leakage from injection wells, leakage during hydrofracking along faults or up abandoned wells, seepage into the ground when wastewater and residuals are applied to land (i.e. used for irrigation or on roads for dust suppression or de-icing), and other means. (US EPA, Science Advisory Board, Hydraulic Fracturing Review Panel, report to Lisa P. Jackson, August 4, 2011).

The cement casing which rings the well bore and goes through underground aquifers is meant to act as a barrier between underground water and the shaft through which frack fluid and gas flow. But the casing can fail or break during the fracturing process, allowing the frack fluid or naturally-occurring contaminants to contaminate groundwater. When that happens, frack fluid and methane can leak from the well bore directly into the water supply, causing dangerous gas buildups, and making water unfit to drink. (Abrahm Lustgarten and ProPublica, "Drill for Natural Gas, Pollute Water," *Scientific American*, 11/17/2008)

Even if the cement casings hold, gas can travel up from the shale layer to the water table. When gas travels through fractures in the rock layer above the shale and in to water supplies, it is called gas migration. (Abrahm Lustgarten and ProPublica, "Does Natural Gas Make Water Burn?" *Scientific American*, 4/27/09)

It is common for wells to lose pressure during the fracking stage, which indicates that the frack fluid is not contained within the well and is seeping into some place the drillers did not anticipate. There has not been enough study of this phenomenon, even though drillers indicate it happens on a frequent basis.

Frack Fluid Disposal

Disposal of the toxic and sometimes radioactive frack fluid is a major logistical problem for fracking companies. When a well is hydraulically fractured, somewhere between 18 and 80 percent of the frack fluid injected into the well will return to the surface. This water, called "flowback" is heavily contaminated by the chemical mixtures that comprise the frack fluid, as well as dissolved salts and heavy metals from deep within the earth. Estimates from the industry indicate that drillers in Pennsylvania created approximately 19 million gallons of this wastewater per day in 2011. The Susquehanna River Basin Commission estimates 20 million gallons per day (MGD) for that same timeframe. ("Permitting Strategy for High Total Dissolved Solids Wastewater Discharges,"4/11/2009)

There is currently no comprehensive set of national standards for the disposal of fracking wastewater.

The presence of certain contaminants commonly found in fracking wastewater—including bromide (which can create toxic by-products) and radionuclides, as well as Total Dissolved Solids (TDS) like salts (for which conventional wastewater treatment is largely ineffective)—are of major concern not only because of the potential impacts on rivers, streams and groundwater, but also for downstream water treatment plants, where conventional treatment technologies are not equipped to deal with such contaminants. According to US EPA, "only a limited number of Publicly Owned Treatment Plants (POTWs) have the ancillary treatment technologies needed to remove the constituents in hydraulic fracturing return waters." (US EPA, Science Advisory Board, Hydraulic Fracturing Review Panel, report to Lisa P. Jackson, August 4, 2011).

Because of lax regulation, fracking companies commonly dispose of contaminated fracking water in the cheapest, easiest ways they can find, regardless of the consequences for communities, water treatment facilities, and the environment. This has led to abuses of waterways and communities close to frack sites.

The *New York Times* reported that in Pennsylvania, wastewater contaminated with radium and other carcinogens was dumped upstream from the intake pipe of a drinking water plant. (Ian Urbina,"Regulation Lax as Gas Wells' Tainted Water Hits Rivers," *New York Times*, 2/26/2011)

Often, wastewater is stored in large evaporation pits, which can off-gas volatile chemicals. Off-gassing is the evaporation of volatile chemicals at normal atmospheric pressure. In 2008, scientists recorded high levels of Volatile Organic Compounds (VOCs) from gas production operations in Colorado, and high levels of wintertime ozone pollution have been linked to oil and gas operations in Wyoming and Utah. (Guyathri Vaidyanathan, "Colo. Plan goes after haze tied to oil and gas operations," E&E Reporter, 3/12/2012; Mark Jaffe, "Like Wyoming, Utah finds high level of wintertime ozone pollution near oil, gas wells," *Denver Post*, 2/26/2012)

The solid waste left over from evaporation pits and land application is treated as ordinary solid waste and exempt from many federal and state regulations, though it can contain toxic residue from the frack fluid. (Ian Urbina, "Recycling of fracking wastewater is no cure-all," *New York Times*, 2/2/2011) Drillers are permitted to apply fracking wastewater residues to roads for de-icing and dust suppression in states like Pennsylvania and New York, and allowed to spray it into the air over tracks of land used for agriculture in Texas.

Fracking Waste Contaminates Groundwater

Gayathri Vaidyanathan

Gayathri Vaidyanathan covers climate science for E&E Publishing's Climatewire. Her work has appeared in the Washington Post, Discover, *and* Nature.

Former EPA scientist Dominic DiGiulio never gave up.

Eight years ago, people in Pavillion, Wyo., living in the middle of a natural gas basin, complained of a bad taste and smell in their drinking water. U.S. EPA launched an inquiry, helmed by DiGiulio, and preliminary testing suggested that the groundwater contained toxic chemicals.

Then, in 2013, the agency suddenly transferred the investigation to state regulators without publishing a final report.

Now, DiGiulio has done it for them.

He published a comprehensive, peer-reviewed study last week in *Environmental Science and Technology* that suggests that people's water wells in Pavillion were contaminated with fracking wastes that are typically stored in unlined pits dug into the ground.

The study also suggests that the entire groundwater resource in the Wind River Basin is contaminated with chemicals linked to hydraulic fracturing, or fracking.

This production technique, which involves cracking shale rock deep underground to extract oil and gas, is popular in the United States. It's also controversial. There are thousands of wells across the American West and in California that are vulnerable to the kind of threat documented in the study, DiGiulio said. He is now a research scholar at Stanford University.

"We showed that groundwater contamination occurred as a result of hydraulic fracturing," DiGiulio said in an interview. "It contaminated the Wind River formation."

The findings underscore the tension at the heart of the Obama administration's climate change policy, which is based on replacing many coal-fired power plants with facilities that burn cleaner natural gas.

That reliance on natural gas has sometimes blinded agencies to local pollution and health impacts associated with the resource, said Rob Jackson, an earth scientist at Stanford and co-author of the study. In 2015, EPA said in a controversial draft study that hydraulic fracturing has not had "widespread, systemic impacts on drinking water resources in the United States" (Greenwire, June 4, 2015).

"The national office of EPA has tended to downplay concerns of their own investigators, in part because the Obama administration has promoted natural gas," Jackson said. "Natural gas is here to stay. It behooves us to make it as safe and environmentally friendly as possible."

EPA spokeswoman Julia Valentine said the agency hasn't yet finalized its assessment that natural gas has no "widespread, systemic impacts." As part of that process, the agency will evaluate all recent research, including DiGiulio's study, she said.

Encana Corp., the company that operated in the Pavillion basin, said repeated testing has shown people's water wells are safe for consumption.

"After numerous rounds of testing by both the state of Wyoming and EPA, there is no evidence that the water quality in domestic wells in the Pavillion Field has changed as a result of oil and gas operations; no oil and gas constituents were found to exceed drinking water standards in any samples taken," said Doug Hock, an Encana spokesman.

Labs can't see fracking chemicals

Water testing began in 2009 when the local EPA office responded to complaints from residents. EPA headquarters, and DiGiulio, got involved in January 2010.

"Conducting a groundwater investigation related to fracking is extremely complicated," DiGiulio said. "It is difficult because a lot of the compounds used for hydraulic fracturing are not commonly analyzed for in commercial labs."

These labs were originally set up for the Superfund program, under which EPA cleans up the most contaminated sites in the nation. They are great at detecting chemicals found at Superfund sites but not as good at detecting chemicals used in fracking, DiGiulio said.

"You have some of these very water-soluble exotic compounds in hydraulic fracturing, which were not amenable to routine lab-type analysis," he said.

One such chemical was methanol. The simplest alcohol, it can trigger permanent nerve damage and blindness in humans when consumed in sufficient quantities. It was used in fracking in Pavillion as workers pumped thousands of gallons of water and chemicals at high pressure into the wells they were drilling. About 10 percent of the mixture contained methanol, DiGiulio said.

So the presence of methanol in the Pavillion aquifer would indicate that fracking fluid may have contaminated it. But methanol degrades rapidly and is reduced within days to trace amounts. Commercial labs did not have the protocol to detect such small traces, so DiGiulio and his colleagues devised new procedures, using high-performance liquid chromatography, to detect it. They devised techniques for detecting other chemicals, as well.

By then, Pavillion was roiling in controversy as EPA and residents collided with industry. EPA had drilled two monitoring wells, MW01 and MW02, in 2011, and its testing had found benzene, diesel and other toxic chemicals. But these results were contested by oil and gas industry representatives, who criticized EPA's sampling techniques (EnergyWire, Oct. 12, 2012). They pointed to a technical disagreement between EPA and the U.S. Geological Survey on the best methods to cast doubt on EPA's overall findings.

EPA realized it needed a consensus on its water testing methodology. In February 2012, it assembled a technical team from the USGS, Wyoming state regulators and tribal representatives from the Wind River Indian Reservation. They retested the monitoring wells in April 2012.

This time, they also tested for methanol. But EPA never released those results to the public. In 2013, the agency backed out of its investigation in Pavillion, handing it over to state regulators, who moved forward using a $1.5 million grant from Encana (EnergyWire, June 21, 2013). DiGiulio said the decision had come from EPA's senior management.

Methanol, diesel and salt

Industry representatives repeatedly pointed out that EPA had not published a peer-reviewed study on its findings.

"If the EPA had any confidence in its draft report, which has been intensely criticized by state regulators and other federal agencies, it would proceed with the peer review process," Steve Everley, a spokesman for Energy in Depth, an industry group, said at the time. "But it's not, which says pretty clearly that the agency is finally acknowledging the severity of those flaws and leaning once again on the expertise of state regulators."

In December 2015, state regulators published a draft of their findings. It stated that fracking had not contributed to pollution in Pavillion, according to the *Casper Star Tribune*. The report said the groundwater is generally suitable for people to use.

When DiGiulio retired from EPA in 2014, he trained his sights on Pavillion. He felt he had to finish his work.

"EPA had basically handed the case over and a peer-reviewed document was never finalized," he said. "If it is not in the peer-reviewed literature, then it presents a problem with credibility in terms of findings. It is important that the work be seen by other scientists and enter the peer review realm so that other scientists will have access to virtually everything."

Since 2012, a trove of new data had accumulated from USGS, EPA and state regulators. He obtained EPA's methanol testing results through a Freedom of Information Act request and downloaded the rest of the information from the Wyoming oil and gas regulator's website. All of it was publicly available, waiting for the right person to spend a year crunching the information.

The end result: a peer-reviewed study that reaffirms EPA's findings that there was something suspicious going on in Pavillion. More research is needed.

The sampling wells contained methanol. They also contained high levels of diesel compounds, suggesting they may have been contaminated by open pits where operators had stored chemicals, DiGiulio said.

The deep groundwater in the region contained high levels of salt and anomalous ions that are found in fracking fluid, DiGiulio said. The chemical composition suggests that fracking fluids may have migrated directly into the aquifer through fractures, he said.

Encana had drilled shallow wells at Pavillion, at depths of less than 2,000 feet and within reach of the aquifer zone, said Jackson of Stanford University.

"The shallow hydraulic fracturing is a potential problem because you don't need a problem with well integrity to have chemicals migrate into drinking water," he said.

The study also shows that there is a strong upward flow of groundwater in the basin, which means contamination that is deep underground could migrate closer to the surface over time.

"Right now, we are saying the data suggests impacts, which is a different statement than a definitive impact," DiGiulio said. "We are saying the dots need to be connected here, monitoring wells need to be installed."

Shallow wells are prevalent

EPA came to the same conclusion in a blistering response last week to Wyoming's draft findings.

"Many of our recommendations suggest that important information gaps be filled to better support conclusions drawn in the report, and that uncertainties and data gaps be discussed in the report," said Valentine, the EPA spokeswoman.

The state had tested people's water wells and detected 19 concerning chemicals. But regulators had concluded that only two chemicals exceeded safe limits and the water could be used for domestic purposes. EPA disagreed. Nearly half the 19 chemicals are unstudied, and scientists do not know the safe level of exposure, EPA stated.

Keith Guille, spokesman for Wyoming's Department of Environmental Quality, declined to comment on DiGiulio's study and on EPA's response to the state's draft report. The state is finalizing its findings and has its eyes set on the future, he said.

"We are not done yet," Guille said.

Energy in Depth, the industry group that had earlier criticized EPA for not publishing a peer-reviewed study, said that DiGiulio's study is "a rehash of EPA's old, discredited data by the very researcher who wrote EPA's original report."

Jackson stressed that the contamination seen at Pavillion could occur in other states where, according to a study published last year in *Environmental Science & Technology* on which he was the lead author, fracking sometimes occurs at shallow depths. That includes the Rocky Mountain region, New Mexico, Colorado, Utah, Montana and California. At present, no state has restrictions on how shallowly a company can frack, he said.

"Shallow hydraulic fracturing is surprisingly common, especially in the western U.S.," Jackson said. "Here in California, half of the wells are fracked shallower than about 2,000 feet."

Given the threat, fracking deserves much greater scrutiny than it has so far received from the Obama administration, said Hugh

MacMillan, a scientist with the environmental group Food and Water Watch.

"Communities have never argued that every well goes bad; they've argued that when you drill and [are] fracking thousands, too many go bad," he said. "For those living on groundwater, it becomes a matter of luck, and that's not right, because over years, more and more people's luck runs out."

EPA Study Identifies Risk of Water Contamination from Fracking

Elizabeth Shogren

Based in Washington, D.C., Elizabeth Shogren covers how major Western issues play out on the national stage.

An investigation by Stanford scientists into a long-simmering controversy finds that hydraulic fracturing did pollute an underground source of drinking water used by people who live near Pavillion, Wyoming, according to a paper published this week in the journal *Environmental Science and Technology*.

The companies that drilled wells over the decades did nothing illegal to cause this problem, which suggests similar undetected contamination may be widespread, according to the scientists.

The scientists base their conclusions on a comprehensive analysis of reams of data available because the tiny rural community has been the scene of one of the highest profile test cases of whether the modern drilling techniques endanger drinking water supplies. In hydraulic fracturing, companies inject large quantities of water, sand and chemicals underground at high pressure to blast open rock or tight sands to get oil or gas flowing.

In several places across the country, people who live near drilling have complained that their well water was newly contaminated with foul odors, rainbow swirls or gases that would easily ignite. But establishing connections between the drilling and the pollution has not been easy. Companies have said the contaminants were naturally occurring or came from other sources.

The Stanford scientists say they are the first to prove the link anywhere in the country. They point to evidence from water samples taken from Environmental Protection Agency monitoring wells near Pavillion. Organic chemicals used in fracking fluids and not

"Fracking linked to groundwater contamination in Pavillion," by Wyoming and Elizabeth Shogren, High Country News, March 30, 2016. Reprinted by permission.

otherwise found in the environment such as methanol, ethanol and isopropanol were detected. "It is the match between chemicals used recently (in hydraulic fracturing and acid stimulation) and what's in the aquifer that is compelling," says Rob Jackson, a Stanford professor of environmental science.

The new research shows that gas wells were not adequately cemented to prevent contaminants from flowing into the aquifer. It also shows that in some cases, hydraulic fracturing and acid stimulation of gas wells took place at depths similar to private drinking water wells, which is not illegal and is more likely to happen in the West because the formations that hold the gas are closer to the surface. The scientists also document that there is no barrier underground such as a layer of impermeable rock to prevent the gas from moving through the aquifer. In other regions of the country, fracking takes place thousands of feet below drinking water wells and impermeable layers of rock block chemicals from moving upwards over time.

The authors' conclusions conflict with a 2015 draft report from the Wyoming Department of Environmental Quality which found that hydraulic fracturing fluids had a "negligible likelihood" of reaching shallower zones used for drinking water.

The Canadian company that produces gas near Pavillion, Encana, criticized the Stanford study. "I would call this speculation or theory," said Doug Hock, a spokesman for Encana. "After numerous rounds of testing by both the state of Wyoming and EPA, there is no evidence that the water quality in domestic wells in the Pavillion field has changed as a result of oil and gas operations."

But the new Stanford study isn't the first to suggest hydraulic fracturing may have sullied groundwater near Pavillion. A 2011 draft report by the EPA was the first to begin to draw the link between hydraulic fracturing and the contaminants in the underground drinking water. As ProPublica and High Country News reported, the agency found suspicious quantities of hydrocarbons and trace contaminants in residents' wells that could be tied to gas development. Then the EPA drilled two 1,000-foot-deep monitoring wells and found high levels of benzene and other carcinogens in the deep groundwater underlying Pavillion. But after much criticism that it had flubbed its research, the agency dropped its study in 2013, and shifted responsibility for further investigation to Wyoming.

Not long after, Dominic DiGiulio, the main researcher of that draft EPA study, retired from the agency and became a visiting scholar at Stanford so he could complete that work. He's the lead author of the new paper.

"We looked at everything we could get our hands on," DiGiulio said in an interview with HCN, including getting data on methanol levels from the EPA through a Freedom of Information Act request. This data helped the scientists show that contaminants from fracking are moving upwards in the aquifer towards where people are getting drinking water.

DiGiulio says he was compelled to complete this "unfinished business" because he believes the problems revealed in Pavillion may be widespread, particularly in the West, where companies conduct hydraulic fracturing in relatively shallow formations to extract coal bed methane and gas locked in tight sands.

"Especially in the Western United States, where it's really dry, there needs to be a better balance" between energy development and the protection of water resources, DiGiulio adds.

Under the 2005 Energy Policy Act, hydraulic fracturing was exempted from the Safe Drinking Water Act. The industry is the only one allowed to inject toxic chemicals into underground formations that may be used for public drinking water. Companies have long contended that they don't contaminate drinking water.

He and Jackson say states or federal government should set limits for how shallow companies can use hydraulic fracturing. No such limits exist. DiGiulio also hopes that the paper will rebut some of the criticisms of his 2011 draft study.

"EPA never responded to any criticisms. It allowed misconceptions to continue. Hopefully this paper will clarify some of that," DiGiulio says.

The authors anticipated criticism, given how much controversy has swirled around Pavillion. As one indication of just how contentious this study is, the journal had it reviewed by seven independent experts, rather than the normal two or three, according to Jackson.

The Stanford scientists concede that their research does not prove that the contamination from fracking goes all the way to domestic wells. What they did prove was that it got into an aquifer that supplies wells and the contaminants are moving upwards, possibly towards wells.

A draft report published in December by the Wyoming Department of Environmental Quality concluded the well water is generally suitable for domestic use, although the levels of some compounds exceeded the EPA's health-based standards.

However, the EPA criticized many aspects of Wyoming's report in an 18-page comment. For example, the EPA found the Wyoming report failed to reflect uncertainties about health risks or to specify when contaminants such as arsenic and uranium were found at much higher levels than would naturally be expected. Some of the uncertainty about health risks stems from the fact that there are no safe drinking water standards for about half of the organic chemicals detected in the drinking water wells, according to the EPA.

The EPA did not have an immediate comment on the Stanford paper but said it would review the findings as part of its final nationwide assessment of the risks of modern drilling techniques for drinking water. The agency's draft assessment showed pathways for contamination but found no evidence of widespread pollution of drinking water.

Controversy Surrounds Wyoming Study of Water Contamination

Scott Tong

Scott Tong is a correspondent for Marketplace's Sustainability Desk, with a focus on energy, environment, resources, climate, supply chain and the global economy.

The potential upsides and downsides of fracking technology for oil and gas keep coming.

The Energy Department found half of all U.S. continental oil production now comes from fracking, bringing enhanced energy self-sufficiency. But injecting wastewater from fracking underground has boosted the risk of earthquakes in parts of Oklahoma and Kansas to the same level as California, according to the U.S. Geology Survey.

Now, a new study focuses on alleged contamination of drinking water in one of the highest-profile, longstanding cases. The location is the small town of Pavillion, Wyoming, population 231.

In 2004, Pavillion resident Louis Meeks said the company Encana drilled for natural gas by his house. And his water changed.

"In our toilets and stuff, we get a yellowish brown stain in there, which never happened til they drilled this well up here," Meeks said. "A lot of times you get in and take a shower and that fine mist will just clear your sinuses."

Meeks and his wife decided to sell their sheep. "We were losing lambs because of this water," he said. "Cows, too. And then our chickens. We have to give them bottled water, or they die."

Controversy has long surrounded Pavillion. The Environmental Protection Agency found that fracking "likely" impacted groundwater in a draft 2011 study, but then discontinued it and handed the study over to the state of Wyoming. The state last December found contamination "unlikely."

This new academic study analyzes all public data on the case, including monitoring wells of the drinking water aquifer.

"We found salts, potassium and chloride that do occur naturally but were much higher than found naturally," said co-author Rob Jackson, an earth system scientist at Stanford University. "We found things like methanol in the water. There was benzene in the water 50 times higher than the allowable levels for drinking water."

The paper concluded fracking had a "clear impact" on drinking water. To Jackson, it also highlights a broader risk: a significant portion of fracking occurs, as it does in Pavillion, at shallow depths, in close proximity to drinking water sources.

"There is no buffer," Jackson said. "The hydraulic fractures open up into the rock. When you're so close, things can migrate into natural cracks and fissures."

The study suggests an additional source of groundwater contamination "impact" in Pavillion: historic pits storing fracking wastewater that were unlined.

One important nuance: the study found fracking chemicals in the groundwater source for household water wells in Pavillion. As for contamination of the actual water wells, the authors found levels concerning, but finding a definitive link requires "further investigation including installation of monitoring wells on the Wind River Formation," according to the paper.

For its part, Encana responded to the study with an emailed statement: "There is no evidence that the water quality in domestic wells in the Pavillion Field has changed as a result of oil and gas operations; no oil and gas constituents were found to exceed drinking water standards in any samples taken."

A spokesman for the state of Wyoming's Department of Environmental Quality told Marketplace the department is busy assessing public comments on its own Pavillion analysis. "We won't have a response to" the Stanford paper, the spokesman said.

On the issue of drilling well integrity, the study found about half the natural gas wells analyzed contained no protective cement below an initial depth. Cementing is designed to protect against fluids or chemicals traveling up the pipe exterior.

"There is no primary cement below surface casing, often for hundreds of meters, for 55 of 106 (52 percent) production wells for which cement bond logs are available," the paper states.

"They weren't completed how they were supposed to be," said Sue Spencer, a hydrogeologist working for Weston Groundwater Engineering in Laramie. "But nobody ever made them go back and fix it, either. Which is weird, because everybody knows that that's a really important thing to do, by the oil industry standards."

For its part, the EPA four years ago abandoned its study of Pavillion and handed it over to Wyoming state regulators. At the time, industry representatives criticized the EPA's data analysis and procedures. Robert Sussman, senior policy counsel at the EPA at the time, told the Casper Star Tribune in December that the agency was on a "collision course" with Encana and Wyoming at the time of its withdrawal.

"There were just serious issues, technical issues about the study," Sussman told the newspaper. "We could spend the next couple of years fighting about the study. Maybe we would win, maybe we would not. We figured staying in this confrontational mode was not going to produce any solutions."

Privately, scientists inside and outside the agency attribute two reasons for the retreat: data collection issues, and political pressure from the White House. The Pavillion withdrawal decision came during the 2012 election campaign, during which President Obama promoted oil and natural production as part of a proposed all-of-the-above energy policy.

Around the same time, the EPA abandoned investigations of alleged fracking contamination in two other cases -- in Parker County, Texas, and Dimock, Pennsylvania.

Separately, the agency has been conducting a national study on the fracking process and risks to drinking water. The study excludes all three high-profile cases in Pavillion, Parker County and Dimock.

"It's so surprising to me that a national multi-year EPA report would almost not mention the most high-profile cases that the EPA was involved with," Jackson said. "It makes no sense."

The EPA's ongoing national study has also drawn attention for its topline finding issued last June in a draft assessment: "Assessment shows hydraulic fracturing activities have not led to widespread systemic impacts to drinking water resources and identifies important vulnerabilities to drinking water resources," an agency press release states.

The draft assessment found "specific instances where one or more mechanisms led to impacts on drinking water resources." A separate EPA "summary of impacts" document provided to Marketplace lists 31 impacts, from blowouts to well failure to frac fluid spills.

Agency scientists in a separate document estimated 600 wells in the country (based on projections) were uncemented below the surface-level casing, based on 2009 and 2010 industry data.

The topline finding of no "widespread systemic impact" is now being questioned by an outside science advisory board (SAB) panel peer-reviewing the EPA draft.

In a draft report to the EPA, the advisory board states: "The SAB finds that this statement does not clearly describe the system(s) of interest (e.g., groundwater, surface water) nor the definitions of 'systemic' and 'widespread.' The SAB agrees that the statement has been interpreted by members of the public in many different ways, and concludes that the statement requires clarification and additional explanation."

Fracking Fluids Do Not Migrate into Drinking Water

Katie Brown

Katie Brown is a communications professional working in the oil and gas industry with extensive on-the-record experience, including print, TV, and radio.

Some of the same researchers who previously claimed that groundwater in the Marcellus region was being contaminated by shale development released a new study this week finding no evidence that hydraulic fracturing fluids have migrated up into drinking water—consistent with what independent scientists and regulators have been saying about fracking for years. The new Proceedings of the National Academy of Sciences study, led by researchers at Yale, includes Robert Jackson (now with Stanford University) and Avner Vengosh, who were both behind the Duke studies that purported to find widespread contamination from shale development. But as their new study explains,

> **We found no evidence for direct communication with shallow drinking water wells due to upward migration form shale horizons.** This result is encouraging, because it implies there is some degree of temporal and spatial separation between injected fluids and the drinking water supply." (p. 5; emphasis added)

This study's finding that contamination is not coming from fracking, but could occur from surface spills, is also not new. In fact, the EPA's five year study of fracking and groundwater released this summer found no evidence for widespread water contamination, and any issues that were identified were isolated and small compared to the total number of wells drilled.

"New Study Finds Fracking Has Not Contaminated Drinking Water," by Katie Brown, Energy In Depth, October 13, 2015. Reprinted by permission. Energy In Depth, a project of the Independent Petroleum Association of America.

Notably, the researchers also ruled out the possibility of well casing failure as a cause of the contamination. From the study,

> Methane abundance from paired samples or previous sampling campaigns showed no correlation with GRO or DRO (SI Appendix, Fig. S4), and the noble gas analysis provided no evidence for fugitive gas contamination in the elevated GRO and DRO samples [e.g., low air-saturated water abundances ([36Ar], [N2]), or 4He/CH4 (10)]. Furthermore, samples with elevated GRO (>5 ppb) had relatively low methane and Br− (<1 ppm for both). **Thus, leaky well casings are an unlikely source of GRO compounds**. (p. 3; emphasis added)

Further, the concentrations of chemicals that the researchers found were "well below" drinking water standards for concern to public health. As the study explains,

> Analyses of purgeable and extractable organic compounds from 64 groundwater samples revealed trace levels of volatile organic compounds, well below the Environmental Protection Agency's maximum contaminant levels, and low levels of both gasoline rans (0-8 ppb) and diesel rang organic compounds (CRO; 0-157 pp). (p. 1)

One of the researchers on the study, Desiree Plata of Yale University, sat down with NPR for an interview in which she explained that the contamination was found "only in a handful of wells." As she put it, "really even using the word contamination is a stretch because when these detections were made they were still at very low concentrations."

Even so, it's worth noting that the study also acknowledges that,

> Organic compounds found in drinking water aquifers above the Marcellus Shale and other shale plays could reflect natural geologic transport processes or contamination from anthropogenic activities, including enhanced natural gas production. (p. 1)

In other words, the researchers point to the possibility that the contamination could be naturally occurring or could have resulted from any industry, not necessarily natural gas development. That's especially important in Pennsylvania because numerous studies using baseline data have found water contamination in wells long before any development. The most recent one comes from a report by researchers at Syracuse University, which looked at 21,000 baseline samples and found,

> no broad changes in variability of chemical quality in this large dataset to suggest any unusual salinization caused by possible release of produced waters from oil and gas operations, even after thousands of gas wells have been drilled among tens of thousands of domestic wells within the two areas studied.

Other studies looking specifically at methane have also found contamination before development ever occurred. Two studies by the U.S. Geological Survey (USGS) found thermogenic methane in water wells in Pennsylvania that predate drilling activity. Another USGS study found high levels of methane in water wells in New York, even though there's a moratorium on fracking.

It's also worth considering the fact that the researchers focus in on the presence of Bis(2-ethylhexyl), which, as they rightly state, is an

> ubiquitous chemical that is used in many industrial practices and materials, and it is difficult to attribute its presence solely to hydraulic fracturing activities. (p. 5)

The researchers explain that they were able to rule out the Bis(2-ethylhexyl) coming from their own analytical procedure but the fact remains that the chemical is contained in a number products. As the Agency for Toxic Substances and Disease Registry explains,

> Di(2-ethylhexyl) phthlate (DEHP) is a manufactured chemical that is commonly added to plastics to make them flexible. DEHP is a colorless liquid with almost no odor. DEHP is present in plastic products such as wall coverings, tablecloths, floor tiles, furniture upholstery, shower curtains, garden hoses, swimming pool liners, rainwear, baby pants, dolls, some toys, shoes, automobile upholstery and tops, packaging film and

sheets, sheathing for wire and cable, medical tubing, and blood storage bags.

This latest study provides a pretty big blow to the anti-fracking groups that have used the Duke researchers' previous research to push their unfounded water contamination claims. For instance, Josh Fox claims writes on his *Gasland* site,

> Industy [sic] arguments that methane occurs naturally in the environment in the Dimock area and therefore should be expected in the water suplly [sic] are dangerously misleading. **A Duke University study found that drilling into the methane layer allows the natural but toxic gas to migrate into the water supply… Additionally, Duke University recently conducted a peer-reviewed study that links water contamination with nearby drilling and fracking, concluding that water wells near drilling and fracking operations were seventeen times more likely to contain elevated levels of methane**. (emphasis added)

Now even the Duke researchers are coming to conclusions very much in line with EPA's findings that hydraulic fracturing does not pose a credible threat to drinking water. It's unfortunate that their previous studies did so much to frighten the public about theoretical risks.

Fracking Does Not Contaminate Aquifers

Brian D. Drollette and Desiree L. Plata

Brian Drollette is a Ph.D. candidate at Yale University researching the impact of natural gas extraction on natural water systems. Desiree Plata is Assistant Professor of Chemical and Environmental Engineering at Yale University. Her research includes industrially-important materials and chemicals and improving development of material and chemical manufacture.

US natural gas production increased by 42% between 2005 and 2014, largely due to recent advances in horizontal drilling and high volume hydraulic fracturing. One of the largest natural gas reservoirs in the US, the Marcellus Shale, underlies much of the state of Pennsylvania, and there is concern that chemicals used in association with gas extraction will end up in local drinking water supplies.

Our study showed that organic chemicals detected in groundwater wells were derived from surface releases (i.e., spills at the ground surface) from hydraulic fracturing operations, rather than transport from deep shale formations. This analysis provides more clarity on potential issues related to hydraulic fracturing and can help communities and industry better address potential water contamination events.

The number of Pennsylvania shale gas wells increased significantly in seven years, and much of that growth was due to unconventional well drilling in the northeastern corner of the state.

"Hydraulic Fracturing Components in Marcellus Groundwater Likely From Surface Operations, Not Wells," by Brian D. Drollette and Desiree L. Plata, The Conversation, October 12, 2015. https://theconversation.com/hydraulic-fracturing-components-in-marcellus-groundwater-likely-from-surface-operations-not-wells-48873.

The bigger picture

To get natural gas from underground shale formations, drillers inject large volumes of water, sand, and some chemicals into wells, which fractures the rock and releases the trapped gas.

Earlier this year, the US Environmental Protection Agency (US EPA) issued a long-awaited assessment of hydraulic fracturing and directly noted "there is insufficient pre- and post-hydraulic fracturing data on the quality of drinking water resources."

Our study helps to address this issue by collecting complimentary geochemical data over a wide geographic area. Nearly 1,000 organic chemicals are disclosed as additives in hydraulic fracturing, but it is unclear if they enter drinking water supplies.

Wastewater from hydraulic fractured wells is collected and disposed of in containment pools or, for permanent disposal, in injection wells.

There are a number of potential migration pathways to groundwater aquifers, including: faulty gas well casings, leaking waste containment ponds, underground fuel storage tanks, migration from deep shale (formations approximately 1 mile deep), and surface releases associated with hydraulic fracturing activities. We determined that the likely exposure pathway was from surface operations at gas well sites and not from deep subsurface transport.

These findings are encouraging, because disclosed spills of chemicals at the surface can be targeted for rapid clean up, and homes in the area can employ point-of-use water treatment technologies when needed. In other words, surface releases are much easier to treat and control than subsurface processes. Also, the types of organic chemicals detected in this study are readily treated by in-home water filtration systems that employ charcoal or activated carbon.

Since domestic fossil fuel production often necessitates the colocation of industrial operations with residential areas, there is an inherent environmental and public health risk associated with accidents, just as with any engineering practice.

Shale gas exploration has increased the area in the US subjected to this type of risk, and efforts to minimize human and machine error will minimize the impacts on local residences. Further, better accident reporting and environmental monitoring can help local municipalities ensure the safety of their drinking water in cooperation with gas extraction experts.

Evidence of fluids

In this study, we focused on over 50 compounds organic compounds associated with hydraulic fracturing to address a gap in research on this topic.

Levels of diesel range organic compounds (hydrophobic chemicals with boiling points similar to diesel fuel) in the groundwater samples were dilute (less than 200 parts per billion). However, they were statistically correlated with distance to the nearest active shale gas well in the region and were significantly higher within a one kilometer radius of a gas well.

These results are similar to studies of hydrocarbon gases (e.g., methane, ethane, and propane) in the same region. In particular, active shale gas wells that have had a documented environmental health and safety violation were spatially correlated with groundwater that contained higher levels of diesel range organic compounds. Furthermore, a known hydraulic fracturing fluid additive, bis(2-ethylhexyl) phthalate, was detected in a subset of samples. This chemical is used in many industrial materials and practices, but it was not detected in a wide range of samples or representative natural water (i.e., a natural spring in the study area).

Upward migration?

A common question regarding the environmental and public health consequences of natural gas extraction via hydraulic fracturing is whether or not fluids can travel from shale horizons to drinking water aquifers through geologic faults and fissures. That is, can hydraulic fracturing fluids migrate upward through cracks to contaminate sources of drinking water?

Proposed upward migration scenarios could introduce the nearly 1000 disclosed organic industrial chemicals used during the fracturing process to shallow groundwater. To date, this remains unproven and undocumented.

The detected organic compounds in the sampled groundwater in our study were not the result of migration of fracturing fluids from the shale horizon to drinking water aquifers. This was demonstrated using a series of complimentary analyses.

For example, fluids migrating from deep shale horizons should contain high amounts of unique noble gases and salts, but the groundwater samples that contained higher diesel range organic compounds did not contain these other chemical markers. In contrast, the chemical character of the groundwater showed the water was in relatively recent contact with the surface of the Earth and was not related to the salt content.

Outstanding questions

Our study focused solely on a region of developed Marcellus Shale in northeastern Pennsylvania, and it is important to note that the results of this study may not translate across all shale formations within the US. Spatial and temporal separations of hydraulically fractured shale horizons can vary widely due to local geology.

Similarly, vertical distances between aquifers and shale formations, as well as the historical oil and gas development in the region, can affect the transport times of deep subsurface fluids to shallow groundwaters. Therefore, continuous monitoring will provide a better understanding of potential risks that may arise over time and space.

Considering that domestic fuel production is growing, it would be helpful to compare the rates of spills associated with natural gas production with spills from other chemical or fuel industries. In ocean transport of oil, only 0.00007% of the volume is released on average (including large spill years). Since gas extraction violation reports do not include volumes, it is not currently possible to answer the question: are surface releases associated with hydraulic fracturing any worse than other fuel technologies on which we rely? Having the volume information will help improve the industrial practices and safety of the growing natural gas industry.

Chapter 4

Will Fracking Lead to Natural Disasters?

Overview: Fracking Is a Boon for Energy Production but May Damage the Environment

Leighton Walter Kille

Leighton Walker Kille writes for Journalist's Resource, a project of the Harvard Kennedy School's Shorenstein Center and the Carnegie-Knight Initiative.

On July 30, 2014, the United States did something that had been legally prohibited for nearly 40 years: It exported domestically produced crude oil. While minor exports had occurred through the years and the July shipment involved some technical sleight-of-hand (the product was classified as lightly refined "condensates"), it was one of the first significant oil shipments since Congress banned exports in the wake of the 1974 oil embargo.

Respecting the law up to now has been easy, given America's declining domestic oil production and thirst for imported oil—in 2006, the country imported 3.7 billion barrels. What changed between then and now all comes down to one word: fracking, the popular name for hydraulic fracturing. Combined with horizontal drilling, the technique has powered a boom in U.S. energy production, unlocking substantial petroleum and natural gas deposits trapped in shale formations. A lot of this is good news: U.S. consumers and industry rarely complain when energy prices fall, and reducing imports from unstable parts of the world has considerable appeal. Natural gas also releases half as much carbon dioxide as coal, allowing it to potentially serve as a "bridge fuel" to the cleaner energy supported by the majority of Americans.

Despite these advantages, fracking remains highly controversial, in large part because of the potential damage it poses to human health and the environment. Reports of fracking operations

"The environmental costs and benefits of fracking: The state of research," by Leighton Walter Kille, Journalist's Resource, October 26, 2014. http://journalistsresource.org/studies/environment/energy/environmental-costs-benefits-fracking.

contaminating aquifers are widespread, and research has found indications of higher rates of silicosis among well workers, an increase in congenital defects to children born nearby, and elevated cancer risk due to air pollution. Even earthquakes have been linked to fracking operations. Such concerns have led a number of towns to try to ban the practice, and fracking has become one of the central issues in the 2014 battle for Colorado's governorship, a crucial swing state.

A 2014 study published in the Annual Reviews of Environment and Resources, "The Environmental Costs and Benefits of Fracking," provides an overview of the state of scientific knowledge on fracking and its impacts. In their introduction, the researchers—based at the Woods Institute for the Environment, Stanford, Duke, Newcastle University, Ohio State, MIT and the University of Colorado—note the complex web of tradeoffs:

> Unconventional energy [recovered by hydraulic fracturing] generates income and, done well, can reduce air pollution and even water use compared with other fossil fuels. Alternatively, it could slow the adoption of renewables and, done poorly, release toxic chemicals into water and air. Primary threats to water resources include surface spills, wastewater disposal, and drinking-water contamination through poor well integrity. An increase in volatile organic compounds and air toxics locally are potential health threats, but the switch from coal to natural gas for electricity generation will reduce sulfur, nitrogen, mercury and particulate air pollution.

The researchers conducted a literature review on a wide range of issues related to unconventional energy, including well productivity, water requirements, well integrity, risks to surface and groundwater, seismic effects, air pollution and greenhouse gasses. In each section the scholars note questions in need of additional research and recommendations. The findings include:

Productivity and reserves

- Based on an analysis of the Barnett Shale in Texas, well production tends to drop sharply after initial fracking. Within five years, wells produce on average just 10% of what they did the first month of operation. Production for wells in the Bakken Shale show a similar rapid decline.
- Initial productivity (IP) rose in the Barnett Shale as companies learned as they went along. They also increased the intensity of extraction, lengthening horizontal drills by 75% and nearly doubling the amount of water used for a single "frack."
- By 2011, productivity of new wells started to decrease as the "sweet spots" were exhausted and subsequent rigs produced less initially and over time. IP fell 22% between 2011 and 2012, despite an additional 10% increase in drilling length.
- Refracturing existing wells can increase the estimated ultimate recovery (EUR) by 30%, but can't reverse their overall decline.
- A 2013 study by the University of Texas of more than 16,000 wells in the state's Barnett Shale region found that its production will peak around 2015, and decline slowly thereafter, and this despite 15,000 more wells being drilled by 2030. This has been called the "Red Queen" syndrome, named after the Alice in Wonderland character who must run faster and faster just to stay in the same place.
- Because fracking is still evolving and estimation of reserves is based on well productivity that can change over time, reserve estimations should be regarded with caution. For example, in 2011 the Energy Information Agency (EIA) estimated that the U.S. had 827 trillion cubic feet of shale gas, but the following year dropped its estimate to 482 trillion cubic feet, a 40% decrease. (Note that some nongovermental organizations have calculated even lower forecasts.)

Water requirements and risks

- Fracking a single well can require anywhere from 2 to 20 million gallons of water, with another 25% used for operations such as drilling and extraction.
- While water use for fracking is in general small relative to agricultural and municipal consumption—it represents less than 1% of total water use in Texas, compared to 56% for crops and 26% for municipalities—it can be quite high in specific areas and time frames. For example, in counties located in the Haynesville, Eagle Ford, and Barnett shales, fracking operations were responsible for 11%, 38%, and 18% of total groundwater use. At its peak, net water use for fracking is projected to increase as much as 136% in the Haynesville Shale, 40% in Barnett and 89% in Eagle Ford.
- The volume of water used per energy generated—known as its water intensity—is lower for fracking than other fossil fuels and nuclear: Coal, nuclear and oil extraction use approximately two, three and ten times, respectively, as much water as fracking per energy unit, and corn ethanol can use 1,000 times more if the plants are irrigated. By comparison, renewables such as wind and photovoltaic solar energy require almost no water.

Well integrity and failure rates

- After the end of a well's operational life, it is "plugged and abandoned" (P&A). In this process, "mechanical or cement barriers, such as packers, at different depths are used to prevent fluids from migrating up or down the well. Improperly abandoned wells provide a short circuit that connects the deeper layers to the surface."
- Publicly available data on well failure rates are still relatively scarce. Pennsylvania State records from 2010 to 2013 indicated that between 3% and 6% of wells in the Marcellus Shale failed. The most extreme form of failure, a blowout, can

cause tremendous damage but is rare: A 2013 study in GeoScienceWorld found that of 3,533 Marcellus wells drilled from 2008 to 2011, only four experienced blowouts.

- One standard measure of how closed wells are performing is "sustained casing pressure" (SCP), an indication that one or more barriers within a well has failed. While it does not always result in environmental contamination, SCP indicates that contamination is possible.
- Rates of sustained casing pressure vary widely: In a survey of 8,000 wells in the Gulf of Mexico approximately 12% showed evidence of SCP, with rates for individual fields varying between 2% and 29%. In Alberta, a survey of 316,000 wells found signs of SCP in 3.9% of them, with one region topping 15%. A 2014 study in Marine and Petroleum Geology found SCP rates "from 3% to 43% of wells in Bahrain, Canada, China, Indonesia, the United Kingdom, the United States, and offshore Norway and the Gulf of Mexico; 12 of 19 studies showed SCP values for ≥10% of wells."

Risks to surface and groundwater

- While it is theoretically possible for fissures created by hydraulic fracturing to connect well bores with shallow aquifers, in practice this is unlikely: Targeted shale formations are generally 1 to 3 kilometers below the surface and the fissures created during operations rarely extend more than 600 meters. In general, contamination through existing fissures or abandoned wells is a "more plausible scenario," as is poor well integrity. (Note that the EPA is investigating a contamination case in Wyoming where the sandstone formation being drilled was as close as 322 meters to the surface in an area with water wells that went as deep as 244 meters.)
- Two studies of the drinking water of a total of 209 homes overlaying the Marcellus Shale in Pennsylvania found

evidence of hydrocarbon pollution. The first study found "17 times higher methane concentrations for the homes," while the second concluded that "casing and cementing issues were the likeliest causes for the fugitive GM that they observed in the shallow aquifers." On the other hand, a study of 127 homes over Arkansas's Fayetteville Shale found no evidence of contamination.

- While the probability of groundwater contamination is "strongly debated and universally controversial," drilling specialists have identified casing and cementing problems as one of their primary environmental concerns.
- Beyond the risk to groundwater supplies, U.S. oil and gas operations generate more than 2 billion gallons of wastewater daily: "These naturally occurring brines are often saline to hypersaline and contain potentially toxic levels of elements such as barium, arsenic, and radioactive radium."
- More than 95% of the wastewater is injected deep underground; other disposal methods are "less common and far less preferable." These include treating it at municipal waste facilities and spraying on public roads for purposes such as dust control. "An experimental application of [approximately] 300,000 liters of flowback water on 0.2 hectares of forest in West Virginia killed more than half the trees within two years."

Seismic effects

- Earthquakes induced by hydraulic fracturing are rare, and those that can be felt by humans are rarer still—only "a handful" of cases have been documented so far, none of greater than 4 Mw. Some cases occur when fracturing is used in areas in existing fracture zones, which are sometimes intentionally targeted because they can result in increased gas production.

- Injection of groundwater can also induce seismic events, and the rate of such events has increased in tandem with unconventional energy extraction: "Between 1967 and 2000, geologists observed a steady background rate of 21 earthquakes of 3.0 Mw or greater in the central United States per year. Starting in 2001, when shale gas and other unconventional energy sources began to grow, the rate rose steadily to [approximately] 100 such earthquakes annually, with 188 in 2011 alone."
- While earthquakes induced by wastewater injection are less frequent than those caused by fracking, their magnitude tends to be greater: "In 2011 alone, earthquakes of 4.0 to 5.3 Mw were linked to deep wastewater injection in locations such as Youngstown, Ohio; Guy, Arkansas; Snyder and Fashing, Texas; and Trinidad, Colorado." The most severe, 5.7 Mw, destroyed 14 homes and injured two people in Oklahoma.

Air pollution

- Unconventional energy extraction is a source of air pollution throughout the preparation, extraction and closure phases. Access roads must be built, the well pad cleared and the bore itself drilled; diesel engines power the fracturing phase. During extraction, wastewater is stored in tanks or open ponds, and any volatile organic compounds (VOCs) are either vented or flared. According to a 2010 study from the U.S. Government Accountability Office (GAO), in 2006 up to 5% of the natural gas production on federal lands in the western United States was lost in this way.
- Atmospheric sampling has indicated even higher rates of escape: A 2013 study in Geophysical Research Letters estimated that in the Uinta Basin of eastern Utah, 55,000 kilograms of methane per hour leak into the atmosphere, the equivalent of 6.2% to 11.7% of total natural gas production in the region.

- Operations related to unconventional energy can also have substantial impacts on air quality: In the Denver basin, more than 6,000 petroleum and condensate tanks are responsible for more than 70% of total VOC emissions from all sources, according to the Colorado Department of Public Health and Environment.
- One of the greatest potential benefits of unconventional energy is the potential for natural gas to displace electrical generation from coal: "Replacing coal with natural gas for power generation would substantially reduce emissions of CO_2, particulate matter (PM), nitrogen oxides (NOx), sulfur dioxide (SO_2), and metals such as mercury (Hg)." However, as stated above, the study does not see worldwide coal consumption falling despite the rise in unconventional energy.

The researchers conclude with five recommendations. First, greater transparency is required from companies and regulating agencies. Some information is available on the FracFocus disclosure registry, but more is needed. Second, short- and long-term studies are required on the potential effects of fracking on operations on human health—"virtually no comprehensive studies have been published on this topic," they note. Third, predrilling data, including environmental quality and human health, would be in all parties' interests. Fourth, because most problems result from surface operations, including faulty wells, spills and leaks, additional work on best practices is required. Finally, funds should be created to address future, unknown problems that could arise from the current oil and gas boom. "Drilling millions of new oil and natural gas wells will inevitably lead to future issues," they note, and authorities and firms should work to ensure that the resources are available to deal with them.

Related research

A 2014 study in Journal of Infrastructure Systems, "Estimating the Consumptive Use Costs of Shale Natural Gas Extraction on Pennsylvania Roadways," analyzes the damage that fracking operations impose on local transportation infrastructure. The researchers, based at the RAND Corporation and Carnegie Mellon University, estimate that the road-reconstruction costs associated with a single horizontal well range from $5,000 to $10,000. While this figure appears small, because there were more than 1,700 wells drilled in Pennsylvania in 2011 alone, the total costs for that year was between $8.5 and $39 million—costs paid by state transportation authorities, and thus taxpayers.

Oil and Gas Industry Activity Causes Earthquakes

Kelly Connelly, David Barer, Yana Skorobogatov

Kelly Connelly reports for KUT News. David Barer and Yana Skorobogatov are with StateImpact Texas and Reporting Texas.

Does Fracking Cause Earthquakes?

Hydraulic fracturing, or "fracking," (a drilling process that injects millions of gallons of water, sand and chemicals under high pressure into a well, cracking the rock and to release natural gas and oil) has only been known to rarely cause earthquakes.

But the disposal of drilling wastewater used in fracking has now been scientifically linked to earthquakes. The fluids used in fracking (and the wastewater that comes back up the well) is disposed of by injecting it into disposal wells deep underground. This is generally regarded as the safest, most cost-efficient way to get rid of it. But in some parts of the country, especially in the Barnett Shale area around Dallas-Fort Worth, it has also been causing earthquakes. And they're growing both in number and strength.

How Fracking Disposal Wells Can Cause Earthquakes

The culprit of earthquakes near fracking sites is not believed to be the act of drilling and fracturing the shale itself, but rather the disposal wells. Disposal wells are the final resting place for used drilling fluid. These waste wells are located thousands of feet underground, encased in layers of concrete. They usually store the waste from several different wells.There are more than 50,000 disposal wells in Texas servicing more than 216,000 active drilling wells, according the the Railroad Commission. Each well uses about 4.5 million gallons of chemical-laced water, according to hydrolicfracturing.com.

"The model I use is called the air hockey table model," says Cliff Frohlich, a research scientist at the Institute for Geophysics at the University of Texas at Austin. "You have an air hockey table, suppose you tilt it, if there's no air on, the puck will just sit there. Gravity wants it to move but it doesn't because there is friction [with the table surface]."

But if you turn the air on for the air hockey table, the puck slips.

"Faults are the same," he says. If you pump water in a fault, the fault can slip, causing an earthquake.

"Scientists in my community know that injection can sometimes cause earthquakes," Frohlich says.

The science linking manmade earthquakes to the oil and gas industry isn't anything new.

Decades ago, researchers even found they could turn earthquakes on and off by injecting liquid into the ground, says Dr. William Ellsworth with the Earthquake Science Center of the U.S. Geological Survey.

"This was seen as validation of the effective stress model," he told StateImpact Texas. "This is work that was published in Science magazine and many other publications."

Recent research has found definitive links between these disposal wells and earthquakes, particularly in Texas.

The quakes are linked to drilling in Barnett Shale. The productive portion of the Barnett Shale is located directly beneath Johnson, Tarrant and western Dallas counties, about a mile and a half underground. The shale contains an estimated 40 trillion cubic feet of natural gas, making it the largest onshore natural gas field in Texas and potentially in the United States.

A University of Texas at Austin from study last summer found a definitive link between earthquakes in the Dallas-Fort Worth area and disposal wells in the Barnett Shale.

And an earlier study by scientists at Southern Methodist University (SMU) and UT found links between disposal wells near the DFW airport and induced earthquakes for a series of quakes in 2008 and 2009. The study specifically looked at two injection wells in the area that were built in 2008. Seven weeks later, earthquakes started. "Were the DFW earthquakes natural or triggered by activities associated with natural gas production, most likely saltwater injection to dispose of brines?" the report asked. The study said yes, the "correlations are consistent with an induced or triggered source."

The quakes studied from that two year period were all 3.0 magnitude or below, but in the years since there have been several quakes above 3.0 in the area, going as high as 3.5. There have been more than fifty earthquakes in the area since 2008.

It's important to note that the earthquakes haven't caused any reported significant damage. Generally an earthquake has to be magnitude 4.0 or higher to cause damage. But locals in the Dallas-Fort Worth area are disturbed and concerned about the trend of manmade seismic activity.

And there's the open question of what kind of damage these induced quakes can do to drilling infrastructure. It's plausible that the tremors could affect well integrity, Frohlich says. "In my business, you never say never. That said, most of the time these earthquakes are not right near the well. But it's possible an earthquake could hurt a well," he says, though he knows of no instances where that's occurred.

It's also important to note that there a tens of thousands of injection and disposal wells in Texas, yet only a few dozen of them are suspected of inducing quakes. It's also true that disposal and injection wells have been known to induce seismic activity since the 1960s. What's happening now is that with the rise of fracking, there is a need for more disposal wells. And in areas where fracking waste water is disposed of near population areas, it's going to be noticed more.

Recent Earthquakes in Texas

South Texas experienced a magnitude 4.8 earthquake in Oct. 2011 near the Eagle Ford Shale Play, which is home to over 550 gas wells. There have been many other earthquakes linked to injection wells in the Dallas-Fort Worth area, over 50 since 2008. There were no earthquakes before then. The most recent quake was 3.0 magnitude on January 22, just outside the DFW airport. You can read about other recent quakes in the stories below.

And the quakes aren't limited to Texas. Ohio experienced a magnitude 4.0 earthquake earlier this year near the town of Youngstown. The *New York Times* reported that Ohio officials believe this quake, the eleventh such event in Youngstown in 2011, was the result of disposal wells. Ohio stores much of Pennsylvania's fracking waste in those wells.

Are the Earthquakes Getting Bigger?

Art McGarr, of the US Geological Survey's Earthquake Science Center, has been looking at whether the amount of fluid stored in a disposal well affects the strength of an earthquake. The question is that as wastewater stays in the disposal wells longer and more and more fluids are added, will the quakes become stronger?

His answer: they will.

"I think we're at the point when, if you tell me that you want to inject a certain amount of waste water, for example a million cubic meters for a particular activity, I can tell you that the maximum magnitude is going to be five (on the rictor scale) or less. I emphasize or less," McGarr said in a recent presentation.

The findings contradict the notion that the rate at which waste fluids are injected in a disposal well impacts the chance of quakes, but it raises another concern. If the findings are correct, they mean the longer a disposal well is injected with fluid, the greater the likelihood of a stronger quake. That means that older wells still in use across Texas and the rest of the country could be growing more and more prone to producing larger earthquakes.

"With time, as an injection activity continues, so will the seismic hazard as measured by the maximum magnitude," said McGarr at the close of his presentation.

Fracking Can Cause Earthquakes, Too

Dr. Cliff Frohlich of the University of Texas at Austin is researching the links between fracking and earthquakes.

Dr. Cliff Frohlich, Associate Director of and Senior Research Scientist at the Institute of Geophysics at the University of Texas at Austin, says that while just a year ago he would have never said fracking itself causes earthquakes, now he thinks differently. "In the last year there have three well-documented earthquakes that occurred during the frack job and were probably related to fracking. They were all small earthquakes—of a magnitude of 2 or 3—and, considering, that there are millions of frack jobs, fracking-related earthquakes are so rare," he told StateImpact Texas.

"The last thing a frack engineer wants is to have the fluids go through a fault and go somewhere," he said. "It's like pouring water through a drain. So if you're a frack engineer's doing their job, they're avoiding faults, and they're trying to bust up area rather than having the fluids move somewhere. People injecting are less concerned about that. They're trying to get rid of it, so they want a very porous material where fluids can flow away across long distances. So they're more likely to get to a fault."

Earthquakes directly linked to fracking have been rare. That hasn't been the case with disposal wells used to get rid of fracking wastewater, however.

What Can Be Done to Prevent Drilling-Related Earthquakes?

Even if the earthquakes aren't getting bigger, the growing scientific link between disposal wells and induced earthquakes has made many residents nervous. In response, some policymakers are searching for solutions.

A report out from the National Research Council referenced a nine year-old checklist of best practices for drillers and disposal well operators. That includes investigating the site's history of earthquakes and its proximity to fault lines. But it included the observation that "government agencies and research institutions may not have sufficient resources to address unexpected (seismic) events."

At a June 2012 Texas House Committee on Energy Resources hearing, state policymakers heard recommendations on what can be done to mitigate the risk of induced earthquakes. Melinda Taylor was one of the experts to give testimony. Taylor directs the Center for Global Energy, International Arbitration, & Environmental Law. She says other states have more safeguards in place against unwanted earthquakes.

In Ohio, for example, well operators need to do a "fairly detailed analysis of the geological conditions" before the state's regulatory agency offers a permit to authorize a new disposal well. "So they can determine whether or not it's likely to cause problems," Taylor says.

What Can Texas Regulators Do?

Taylor also said the Texas Railroad Commission, which regulates oil and gas drilling in the state, may want to consider mandating setbacks, to ensure greater distance between disposal wells and public drinking water supplies, structures, and natural resources.

But as StateImpact Texas reported in January 2013, Texas regulators are largely ignoring the problem.

In a December 2012 forum hosted by the Texas Tribune, Railroad Commission Chair Barry Smitherman said he was aware of what he called "allegations" of a link between disposal wells and quakes.

"I know there are a number of studies being done and I think the University of Texas is doing one, and I'm anxious to see what kind of results we're going to get," he said in response to a question from StateImpact Texas. That study was released several months before, in August 2012.

That 'wait and see' approach is very close to the public position the Commission has taken previously. In an email to StateImpact Texas, Commission spokesperson Ramona Nye wrote that staff welcomes more data about "theories that hypothesize" a causation between seismic events and injection wells. But the Commission would not make any staff members available for interview.

To figure out how seriously the Commission was taking man-made earthquakes, StateImpact Texas filed open records requests for Commission emails relating to the subject.

The 111 pages of emails the Commission supplied show that staff members there accept what scientists and oilmen have known for decades: Injection wells can cause earthquakes. They even show staff members in communication with EPA researchers over certain quakes. The messages include forwards of media reporting on earthquakes and notes of concern from Texans.

Then the emails stop.

The last email about earthquakes that the Railroad Commission has on record was dated August 6, 2012. There was no record of electronic communication about the quakes that hit the Dallas area in late September, nor about quakes that hit North Texas in October, November or December.

The Railroad Commission is starting the process of writing new rules about disposal wells. But in an email to StateImpact Texas, the Commission said those proposed amendments "do not address seismic activity."

Frolich, the UT expert on man-made earthquakes, had one last suggestion on how to mitigate unwanted quakes: find new ways of disposing drilling related wastewater.

"If disposal is causing earthquakes you can find a different way of dispose of it. You can dispose of the stuff in a different well, or you can even take it to a fluid treatment plant," Frolich said.

Of course, companies' willingness to do that will depend largely on cost and state regulation.

"The people involved in this [disposal well operation] are going to do the cheapest way of doing things that is generally considered safe," said Frolich.

Fracking Causes Earthquakes

Matthew Hornbach

Matthew Hornbach is Associate Professor of Geophysics at Southern Methodist University. His research focuses on heat flow and fluid modeling; paleoseismology and geohazards; marine geology and geophysics; and gas hydrates.

If you've been following the news lately, chances are you've heard about—or even felt—earthquakes in the central United States. During the past five years, there has been an unprecedented increase in earthquakes in the North American mid-continent, a region previously considered one of the most stable on Earth.

According to a recent report by the Oklahoma Geological Survey, Oklahoma alone has seen seismicity rates increase 600 times compared to historic levels.

The state has gone from experiencing fewer than two magnitude-three earthquakes per year to greater than two per day, the report found. Similarly, my home state of Texas has experienced a near 10-fold increase in magnitude-three earthquakes or greater in the past five years.

The recent uptick in earthquakes in Texas, Oklahoma and several other central US states raises an obvious question: What is causing all of this seismicity?

Earthquake Causes

Several factors can promote the occurrence of earthquakes. There are natural changes caused by the shifting of Earth's plates, the advance and retreat of glaciers, the addition or removal of surface water or ground water, and the injection or removal of fluids due to industrial activity.

Studies including two reports issued in April, indicate that human activities, including activities related to oil and gas extraction, are beginning to play a significant role in triggering earthquakes in the central US.

Extracting oil and gas from shale rock involves cracking, or fracturing, a layer of underground rock with a high-pressure mix of water, sand, and chemicals. As the oil and gas are released, those injection fluids and briny water also come up. That wastewater is later disposed of in what are called injection wells, or sometimes disposal wells.

It is important to note that it is not the fracking process itself that usually causes these earthquakes; it is the rapid injection of fluid during wastewater disposal that sometimes pumps hundreds of millions of gallons of brine deep into the earth each year.

Hundreds of Studies

So do injection wells cause earthquakes?

A recent peer-reviewed scientific study I co-authored concludes human-activities, specifically water production and wastewater injection, represent the most likely cause of earthquakes in the Azle/Reno, Texas region, where significant gas production and wastewater injection began five years ago.

But this is not a fundamentally new discovery. For nearly a century, industry and academic researchers have recognized that human activities can and do sometimes trigger earthquakes.

Indeed, entire books—including many standard texts used in advanced petroleum geology, geomechanics, and petroleum engineering classes—are dedicated to understanding fault reactivation, rock mechanics, and the ways humans can facilitate these processes for the betterment of humanity.

Additionally, multiple studies and reports, including hundreds of peer-reviewed scientific studies—and independent studies conducted by the National Research Council of the United States National Academy of Science and Engineering—confirm that the injection or removal of fluids can and indeed do trigger earthquakes.

What is unique and exciting about our Azle/Reno study is the unprecedented support and cooperation of the energy industry, which in many instances provided mission-critical data, technical support, and constructive scientific reviews to allow scientists to better assess, model, and understand earthquakes in the Azle/Reno area and across Texas.

In our instance, industry researchers went far beyond state regulatory requirements by providing insight into the location and orientation of regional faults, injection reservoir pressures, and subsurface flow.

The Azle/Reno study highlights how cooperation, transparency, and mutual respect between, industry, academia, and regulators can improve our understanding of seismicity, and help mitigate risk for all parties working, living, and conducting business in Texas.

Can This Risk Be Mitigated?

Human-triggered earthquakes often involve the rapid removal or injection of large volumes of liquids from the surface, or subsurface.

As our study, and many studies—including those conducted by industry—suggest, the key to understanding and mitigating earthquake hazards in Texas and elsewhere is high-quality data, especially data that monitor and assess subsurface pressures, fluid injection volumes, fluid extraction volumes, and regional seismicity with time.

A recent US Geological Survey (USGS) report indicates the seismic hazard in some areas of Texas is now comparable to areas of Oklahoma and California due in part to wastewater injection.

That said, it is equally important to note that thousands of injection wells exist across Texas (and other states) that have no associated felt seismicity. Indeed, at this time, only a tiny minority of injection wells in Texas have been plausibly linked to earthquakes.

Although the rate of seismicity in Texas has clearly accelerated in the past five years, it is still very low across much of the state. This is also generally true for Arkansas, Ohio, Colorado, and

Kansas, where links have been suggested between disposal wells and earthquakes.

In short, now is not a time to panic, but a time to take stock of the resources available to make well-informed science-based decisions that allow states to understand, prepare, and mitigate risk associated with earthquake hazards.

Indeed, scientists are actively researching how to better understand and ultimately reduce human-triggered earthquakes.

There have been studies to develop a general hazard model for injection wells as well as specific strategies on how to reduce risk during and prior to the injection process. These strategies generally include the early detection and location of potentially weak faults, choosing appropriate injection reservoirs that minimize the risk of increasing underground pressure, and adjusting wastewater injection practices to reduce or minimize seismicity.

Scientists can also collect more detailed brine production and injection data, underground pressure data, and regional seismic data to better predict how subsurface pressures and associated seismicity might evolve with time. These techniques are already being implementing at known induced seismicity sites with success.

History dictates that the advent of new technology often leads to new and unforeseen challenges. The printing press, the automobile, and splitting the atom have provided incalculable benefits to humanity but also incredible responsibility.

What is recognized as the Texas-led "Shale Revolution," arguably one of the most significant innovations of the modern era, is no different.

Our society is blessed with some of the finest scientists and engineers in all of industry and academia. Working together, with support from regulatory agencies, we believe the same scientific prowess, ingenuity, and entrepreneurial spirit that advanced the hydrocarbon industry in the US this past decade can also help address the new challenges and responsibilities emerging.

There Is Little Scientific Evidence Linking Fracking to Earthquakes

Marita Noon

Marita Noon, the author of Energy Freedom, is executive director of Energy Makes America Great Inc. and the companion educational organization, Citizens' Alliance for Responsible Energy (CARE).

People in seven states, from South Dakota to Texas, were awakened Saturday morning, September 3, by Oklahoma's most powerful earthquake in recorded history. The 5.8 tremor was centered near Pawnee, OK. Several buildings sustained minor damage and there were no serious injuries.

That we know.

What we don't know is what caused the quake—but that didn't stop the alarmist headlines from quickly blaming it on "fracking."

Green Party candidate Dr. Jill Stein promptly tweeted: "Fracking causes polluted drinking water + earthquakes. The #GreenNewDeal comes with none of these side effects, Oklahoma. #BanFracking"

A headline in *Forbes* stated: "Thanks to fracking, earthquake hazards in parts of Oklahoma now comparable to California."

The *Dallas Morning News* proclaimed: "Oklahoma shuts down fracking water wells after quake rattles Dallas to Dakotas."

NaturalNews.com questions: "Was Oklahoma's recent record breaking earthquake caused by fracking?"

A report from ABC claims: "The increase of high-magnitude earthquakes in the region has been tied to the surge in oil and gas operators' use of hydraulic fracturing, or fracking…"

Citing a March 2016 report from the U.S. Geological Survey (USGS) on "induced earthquakes," CNN says: "The report found that oil and gas drilling activity, particularly practices like hydraulic fracturing or fracking, is at issue. Saturday's earthquake spurred

"Fracking Is Not Causing Earthquakes," Natural Gas NOW, naturalgasnow.org. Reprinted by permission.

state regulators in Oklahoma to order 37 disposal wells, which are used by frackers, to shut down over a 725-square mile area."

Despite these dramatic accusations, the science doesn't support them. The USGS website clearly states: "Fracking is NOT causing most of the induced earthquakes." An important study from Stanford School of Earth, Energy & Environmental Sciences on the Oklahoma earthquakes, which I wrote about last year, makes clear that they are "unrelated to hydraulic fracturing."

While the exact cause of the September 3 quake is still undetermined, geologists close to the research do not believe it is fracking related. (Realize 5.5 El Reno earthquake, centered near the western edge of Oklahoma City, in 1952 was from natural causes.) At a September 8 meeting on Seismicity in Oklahoma, according to Rex Buchanan, Interim director of the Kansas Geological Survey: "There was relatively little conversation about fracking and far more conversation about wastewater."

William Ellsworth, Professor (Research) of Geophysics at Stanford University, told me that while no specific information about this direct case is available: "I don't have any information that would allow me to rule out fracking. However, it is extremely unlikely. Fracking occurs for a few days at most, if at all, when the well is being finished. Wastewater injection goes on continuously for years and years."

The error in the reporting occurs, I believe, because people don't generally understand the difference between drilling and hydraulic fracturing, and produced water and flowback water, and, therefore, merge them all into one package.

Yes, it does appear that the increase in induced, or human-caused, earthquakes may be the result of oil-and-gas development, yet totally banning fracking, as Stein and Hillary Clinton support, would not diminish the tremors.

First, not every oil or gas well is drilled using hydraulic fracturing. As Ellsworth mentioned, fracking is a part of the process used on some wells. However, much of the drilling done in the part of Oklahoma where the seismic activity first occurred is conventional and doesn't involve fracking—which provided a premise for the Stanford researchers' study.

When a well uses the hydraulic fracturing enhanced recovery technology, millions of gallons of water, plus sand and chemicals, are pumped into the well at high pressure to crack the rock and release the resource. When the oil or gas comes up from deep underground, the liquids injected come back to the surface too. This is called flowback water. That water is separated from the oil and/or gas and may be reused, recycled (as I wrote about in December), or disposed of in deep wells known as injection wells—which are believed to be the source of the induced seismic activity.

"Ha!" you may think, "See, it is connected to fracking." This brings the discussion to produced water—which is different from flowback water.

This type of wastewater is produced at nearly every oil and gas extraction well—whether or not it is fracked. The water, oil, and gas are all "remnants of ancient seas that heat, pressure and time transformed," explains Scott Tinker, Texas' state geologist and director of the University of Texas at Austin's Bureau of Economic Geology. He continues: "Although the water is natural, it can be several orders of magnitude more saline than seawater and is often laced with naturally occurring radioactive material. It is toxic to plants and animals, so operators bury it deep underground to protect drinking-water supplies closer to the surface." In Oklahoma, the wastewater is often injected into the Arbuckle formation.

While the hydraulic fracturing process is typically only a few days, the produced water can be brought to the surface with the oil and/or gas for years. With the increased oil and gas extraction in the past several years—before the 2014 bust, the volumes of wastewater also soared. In parts of Oklahoma, ten barrels of wastewater are produced with every barrel of oil. Scientific American reports that some of those high-volume injection wells "absorbed more than 300,000 barrels of water per month."

The authors of the Stanford study were "able to review data about the amount of wastewater injected at the wells as well as the total amount of hydraulic fracturing happening in each study area, they were able to conclude that the bulk of the injected water was produced water generated using conventional oil extraction techniques, not during hydraulic fracturing," writes Ker Than for Stanford. Professor Mark Zoback, lead author of the study states: "We know that some of the produced water came from wells that were hydraulically fractured, but in the three areas of most seismicity, over 95 percent of the wastewater disposal is produced water, not hydraulic flowback water." Ellsworth agrees. Last year, he told the Associated Press: "The controversial method of hydraulic fracturing or fracking, even though that may be used in the drilling, is not physically causing the shakes."

So, if banning fracking won't stop the shaking, what will? The geologists contacted for this coverage agree that more work is needed. While the quakes seem to be connected to the wastewater injection wells, there are thousands of such wells where no discernable seismic activity has occurred. Oklahoma has been putting new restrictions on some of its thousands of disposal wells for more than a year to curb seismic activity and that, combined with reduced drilling activity due to low prices, has reduced the rate of the tremors. In Texas, when the volumes of wastewater being injected into the vicinity of that state's earthquakes were reduced, the earthquakes died down as well. Other mitigation strategies are being explored.

Jeremy Boak, director, Oklahoma Geological Survey, told me: "The Oklahoma Geological Survey is on record as concluding that the rise from 1-2 M3.0+ earthquakes per year to 579 (2014), 907 (2015) and the current 482 (to date in 2016) are largely driven by increased fluid pressure in faults in the basement driven largely by injection of water co-produced with oil and gas and disposed of in the Arbuckle Group, which sits on top of basement. Both the increase and the current decreasing rate appear to be in response to changes in the rate of injection. There are natural earthquakes in Oklahoma, but the current numbers dwarf the inferred background rate."

Interestingly, most of the aforementioned reports that link fracking and earthquakes, ultimately acknowledge that it is the wastewater disposal, not the actual hydraulic fracturing, that is associated with the increased seismic activity—but, they generally fail to separate the different types of wastewater and, therefore, make the dramatic claims about fracking.

Boak emphasized: "There are places where there are documented cases of earthquakes on individual faults occurring very near and during hydraulic fracturing operations, including one published case in Oklahoma. These are generally small earthquakes, although some larger ones (M4.0+) have occurred in British Columbia. Therefore, it is technically very important to maintain the distinction between injection-induced and hydraulic fracturing-induced earthquakes, or we may take the wrong action to solve the problem. Should the OGS and Oklahoma Corporation Commission (OCC) staff find further Oklahoma examples of such earthquakes, the OCC will take action. The current issue of injection-induced seismicity must take precedence."

When you hear supposedly solid sources blaming hydraulic fracturing for earthquakes, remember the facts don't support the accusations. Fracking isn't causing Oklahoma's increased earthquakes.

Experts Say Fracking Not the Cause of Oklahoma Earthquakes

Seth Whitehead

Seth Whitehead is a spokesman for Energy In Depth, an education and research program sponsored by the Independent Petroleum Association of America.

Experts really could not be clearer: They have said over and over that the fracking process is not the cause of earthquakes in Oklahoma.

The United States Geological Survey (USGS) states in the very first sentence of its list of myths and misconceptions regarding induced seismicity that "Fracking is NOT causing most of the induced earthquakes," further clarifying that "Wastewater disposal is the primary cause of the recent increase in earthquakes in the central United States."

Stanford geophysicist Mark Zoback explains in a recent YouTube video, quite bluntly, that Oklahoma's induced seismicity "… is not caused by the hydraulic fracturing process at all."

Still, the false notion that fracking causes earthquakes prevails—and many media outlets' coverage of the 5.6-magnitude earthquake near Pawnee, Okla., over Labor Day weekend is the prime example why.

Headlines such as Newsweek's "Oklahoma's 5.6 Magnitude Earthquake Sparks Fracking Fears" and the *Dallas Morning News*' "Oklahoma shuts down fracking water wells after quake rattles Dallas to Dakotas" stand out. Bloomberg even had three separate articles in which erroneous headlines and claims abound.

To their credit, some reporters such as Mike Soraghan of E&E News, Doug Stanglin of *USA Today* and Jim Malewitz from the

Texas Tribune made a point to emphasize that fracking is not the cause. As E&E News even reported:

> **Scientists have not linked the earthquake swarms to "hydraulic fracturing," in which chemical-laced water is forced downhole at high pressure to crack rock and release oil and gas.** Fracturing creates wastewater, but studies have indicated that flowback from the "fracking" process is only a small part of the water being disposed of. Instead, most of the water comes from ongoing production from shale, conventional and other types of production. (emphasis added)

Here is a look at the most erroneous claims made by several media outlets, followed by the facts.

Dallas Morning News Claim

"The state ordered operators to significantly reduce the volume of wastewater from production that they pump into wells. The process, known as hydraulic fracturing or fracking, involves injecting wells with water, sand and chemicals at high pressure to fracture rock and release oil and natural gas. That also brings up fracking fluid and salty groundwater."

Here the *Dallas Morning News* clearly doesn't know the difference between injection and fracking—even though they are completely different processes—and is determined to make fracking the culprit. But the overwhelming consensus of actual experts is that this is simply not true. We highlighted a pair of examples earlier, but that's just the tip of the iceberg.

Here's what leading geologists, geophysicists, and engineers—rather than click-bait happy media outlets looking for any excuse to get the word "fracking" in a headline—have stated with regard to fracking causing earthquakes.

- Former Interior Department Deputy Secretary David Hayes has said "We also find that there is **no evidence** to suggest that hydraulic fracturing itself is the cause of the increased rate of earthquakes."

- University of Texas at Austin Geophysicist Cliff Frohlich has said "Although there is a considerable amount of hydraulic fracturing activity in the Eagle Ford, we don't see a strong signal associated with that and earthquakes."
- A 2012 Inglewood oil field study concluded "High-volume hydraulic fracturing…had no detectable effects on vibration, and did not induce seismicity (earthquakes)
- A Durham University study found ""…after hundreds of thousands of fracturing operations, only three examples of felt seismicity have been documented. The likelihood of inducing felt seismicity by hydraulic fracturing is thus **extremely small**…"
- The National Research Council—part of the prestigious National Academies —has similarly found: "The process of hydraulic fracturing a well as presently implemented for shale gas recovery does not pose a high risk for inducing felt seismic events."
- And, as USGS noted in a separate report than the one referenced earlier: "USGS's studies suggest that the actual hydraulic fracturing process is only very rarely the direct cause of felt earthquakes. While hydraulic fracturing works by making thousands of extremely small 'microearthquakes,' they are, with just a few exceptions, too small to be felt; none have been large enough to cause structural damage." (emphasis added)

Zoback has put the latter in point in proper perspective, saying "It is important to note that the extremely small microseismic events occur during hydraulic fracturing operations. These microseismic events affect a very small volume of rock and release, on average, about the same amount of energy as a gallon of milk falling off a kitchen counter."

ABC News Claim

Operators were asked to shut down "wells that gather wastewater from a process called hydrofracturing or fracking."

FACT: Some outlets would have readers believe that wastewater from the actual fracking process—known as fracking flowback water—is the only wastewater that is disposed of in injection wells. But the near polar opposite is true.

The overwhelming majority of oil and gas-related wastewater disposed in Oklahoma injection wells is from day-to-day production—not the fracking process.

A recent Zoback study on Oklahoma's induced seismicity actually found that more than 95 percent of wastewater disposed of in Oklahoma's most seismically active areas is produced water, or brine, from day-to-day production. The study's press release states,

> We know that some of the produced water came from wells that were hydraulically fractured, but in the three areas of most seismicity, over 95 percent of the wastewater disposal is produced water, not hydraulic fracturing flowback water.

The USGS induced seismicity fact sheet concurs with the Zoback study's findings:

> In many locations, wastewater has little or nothing to do with hydraulic fracturing. In Oklahoma, less than 10 percent of the water injected into wastewater disposal wells is used hydraulic fracturing fluid. Most of the wastewater in Oklahoma is saltwater that comes up along with oil during the extraction process.

Fact is, high volumes of wastewater injection far pre-date fracking in the Sooner State. Wastewater injection wells have been widely used in Oklahoma for more than a half a century and are in no way a new technology that has somehow been made necessary by the rise of high volume, horizontal hydraulic fracturing in the 2000s.

Bloomberg Claim

"Oklahoma, a region not known for seismic activity, began having earthquakes in 2009, the same year area oil companies began using fracking to shatter deep rock layers to extract oil and gas."

Fact: Bloomberg suggests fracking is the cause when overwhelming expert consensus has determined wastewater injection is the likely culprit. And the notion that fracking directly resulted in more wastewater doesn't hold up to scrutiny, either.

Produced wastewater volumes in Oklahoma were actually about 30 percent higher in the 1980s than they have been in recent years, yet there were only a handful of recorded earthquakes in Oklahoma during that earlier time. Data are sparse for that period, and some scientists have suggested that much of the water may have been injected into wells used for enhanced oil recovery (EOR). Regardless, this underscores the fact that any link between wastewater injection and seismicity is highly complex, and due to a variety of factors that are often site-specific.

This is one reason experts have been somewhat mystified regarding the sudden spike in induced seismicity in a state in which high volumes of wastewater have long been disposed of via injection wells. Tim Baker, director of the Oil and Gas Conservation Division of the Oklahoma Corporation Commission, alluded to this fact in this recent YouTube video regarding induced seismicity in Oklahoma stating "close to 10,000 wells" were injecting wastewater in Oklahoma before high volume fracking was used in the state. Roughly 4,200 injection wells are being used today.

On that point, it's worth remembering that experts are still working to determine if there is a link between injection wells and the quake that happened over Labor Day weekend. As the USGS explained,

> Without studying the specifics of the wastewater injection and oil and gas production in this area, the USGS cannot currently conclude whether or not this particular earthquake was caused by industrial-related, human activities," the USGS said in a statement. "However, we do know that many earthquakes in Oklahoma have been triggered by wastewater fluid injection.

The USGS will continue to process seismic data in the coming days and weeks "that will help answer this question," it added.

Conclusion

Though significant and certainly worthy of concern, the earthquake near Pawnee over Labor Day weekend should not overshadow the fact that earthquakes in Oklahoma were down 52 percent between January and April of this year, according to data from the Oklahoma Geological Survey.

It's also important to note that this decline occurred while oil and gas production in Oklahoma remained relatively unchanged—and the recent drop in seismicity has come without a ban or moratorium on wastewater disposal in the state—something many activists have argued would be the only solution.

Since last summer, the OCC has implemented more than a dozen directives and other measures in response to earthquake activity. The plans have included increased monitoring, well plugging, and volume reductions for hundreds of injection sites near seismic events.

And the Oklahoma Corporation Commission immediately took action after the Pawnee-area quake, indefinitely shutting down 37 disposal wells in a 500-square miles area of interest surrounding the epicenter over a 10-day period (wells within a five-mile radius in five days), continuing the proactive approach that has yielded declines in seismic activity so far this year.

The OCC's firm yet proactive actions have been rooted in the fact that wastewater injection is a process that has been used safely since the 1930s and deemed safe by the U.S. Environmental Protection Agency. For good reason: induced seismicity has been linked to a very small percentage of wastewater injection wells—Oklahoma included—and such a ban would effectively shut down all oil and gas production in any state with significant oil and gas production.

If activists had their way, a ban on all wastewater injection would be particularly devastating to Oklahoma, a state in which the oil and natural gas industry has accounted for nearly two-thirds of all jobs created in the state since 2010, according to an economist at Oklahoma City University. The industry is also the "largest single source of tax revenue" in the state, according to a 2014 report prepared for the State Chamber of Oklahoma. Over 20 percent of all state taxes come from the oil and natural gas industry.

Understanding these realities is key to understanding the issue of wastewater injection and induced seismicity—particularly with how they relate to the actual fracking process, which is why Zoback has said,

> I really think bans on hydraulic fracturing are political statements rather than risk management tools.

Unfortunately, the sort of misinformation being pushed by media reports continue to exacerbate the general misunderstanding of the very complicated issue of induced seismicity—which has been inaccurately linked directly to fracking—prompting Southern Methodist University (SMU) professor Matthew Hornbach to say the following,

> We're not talking at all about fracking. In fact, it's been driving us crazy, frankly, that people keep using it in the press.

Organizations to Contact

The editors have compiled the following list of organizations concerned with the issues debated in this book. The descriptions are derived from materials provided by the organizations. All have publications or information available for interested readers. This list was compiled on the date of publication of the present volume; the information provided here may change. Be aware that many organizations take several weeks or longer to respond to inquiries, so allow as much time as possible.

Americans Against Fracking
website: www.americansagainstfracking.org/

Fracking and drilling associated with fracking pose a direct and immediate threat to the drinking water, air, climate, food, health and economies of communities across the United States. Americans Against Fracking is comprised of entities dedicated to banning drilling and fracking for oil and natural gas in order to protect our shared vital resources for future generations.

American Gas Association
400 North Capitol Street, NW, Suite 450, Washington, DC 20001
(202) 824-7000
website: www.aga.org/

The American Gas Association, founded in 1918, represents more than 200 local energy companies that deliver clean natural gas throughout the United States. There are more than 73 million residential, commercial and industrial natural gas customers in the U.S., of which 95 percent—more than 69 million customers—receive their gas from AGA members. Today, natural gas meets more than one-fourth of the United States' energy needs.

Center For Responsible Shale Development

625 Liberty Avenue, Suite 395, Pittsburgh, PA 15222
(412) 804.4170
email: info@responsibleshaledevelopment.org
website: responsibleshaledevelopment.org

The Center for Responsible Shale Development is a non-profit organization whose vision is to bring together environmental and gas industry leaders committed to driving continuous innovation and improvement of shale development practices within the Appalachian Basin.

Earth Justice

50 California Street, Suite 500, San Francisco, CA 94111
(800) 584-6460
Fax: (415) 217-2040
email: headquarters@earthjustice.org
website: earthjustice.org

As the nation's original and largest nonprofit environmental law organization, Earth Justice leverages expertise and commitment to fight for justice and advance the promise of a healthy world for all. We represent every one of our clients free of charge.

Energy In Depth

1201 15th Street NW, Suite 300, Washington, DC 20005
(202) 346-8845
email: energyindepth@energyindepth.org
website: energyindepth.org

Launched by the Independent Petroleum Association of America (IPAA) in 2009, Energy In Depth (EID) is a research, education and public outreach campaign focused on getting the facts out about the promise and potential of responsibly developing America's onshore energy resource base—especially abundant sources of oil and natural gas from shale and other "tight" formations across the country.

Environmental Protection Agency (EPA)
1200 Pennsylvania Avenue, N.W., Washington, DC 20460
(888) 372-7341
website: www.epa.gov

The EPA's purpose is to ensure that all Americans are protected from significant risks to human health and the environment where they live, learn and work.

Global Frackdown
email: http://www.globalfrackdown.org/contact-us/
website: www.globalfrackdown.org

Since 2012, the Global Frackdown—an international day of action initiated by Food & Water Watch to ban fracking—has helped connect activists across the globe and demonstrated the growing power of the movement to stop fracking, gas infrastructure, sand mining and other related extraction methods. This movement is fueled by increasing scientific evidence of the impact of fracking on water, air, health, seismic stability, communities, and the climate on which we all depend.

Indigenous Environmental Network
PO Box 485, Bemidji, MN 56619
(218) 751-4967
website: www.ienearth.org

Established in 1990 within the United States, IEN was formed by grassroots Indigenous peoples and individuals to address environmental and economic justice issues (EJ). IEN's activities include building the capacity of Indigenous communities and tribal governments to develop mechanisms to protect our sacred sites, land, water, air, natural resources, health of both our people and all living things, and to build economically sustainable communities.

Marcellus Protest
c/o Thomas Merton Center, 5129 Penn Avenue, Pittsburgh, PA 15224

(724) 485-9835
email: info@marcellusprotest.org
website: marcellusprotest.org

MarcellusProtest.org is an information clearing house about Marcellus Shale gas drilling and activism and related issues. Although this website's primary geographic focus is Western Pennsylvania, MarcellusProtest.org also includes content pertaining to the five states in which the Marcellus Shale is located—as well as other Shale gas formations across the U.S. A new social movement is in the making, and it's going national.

North Texans for Natural Gas

website: www.northtexansfornaturalgas.com/about

North Texans for Natural Gas is a grassroots organization that aims to give a voice to those who support natural gas. We are proud of all that natural gas has done for our community and the significant benefits it brings to our economy, schools, and neighborhoods.

Stop the Frack Attack

website:www.stopthefrackattack.org

Stop the Frack Attack's goals are: To be a movement hub that acts as a centralized place to coordinate with other groups working on oil and gas drilling using the fracking process. To ensure impacted community members are given a meaningful seat at the table and are respected, trusted, and consulted. To facilitate and coordinate trainings and leadership development of community member. To push for a transformative organizing model, that looks as issues as a whole and their connections to issues of oppression.

Bibliography

Books

Michelle Bamberger and Robert Oswald. *The Real Cost of Fracking: How America's Shale Gas Boom Is Threatening Our Families, Pets, and Food*. Boston, MA: Beacon Press, 2014.

Blaire Briody. *The New Wild West: Black Gold, Fracking, and Life in a North Dakota Boomtown*. New York, NY: St. Martin's Press, 2017.

Adam Briggle. *A Field Philosopher's Guide to Fracking: How One Texas Town Stood Up to Big Oil and Gas*. New York, NY: Liveright Publishing Corp, 2015.

Chris Faulkner. *The Fracking Truth:America's Energy Revolution: America's Energy Revolution: the Inside, Untold Story*. Doylestown, PA: Platform Press, 2014.

Eric George and Jacqueline George. *Fracking 101: A Beginner's Guide to Hydraulic Fracturing*. Australia: Q Press Publishing, 2016.

Russell Gold. *The Boom: How Fracking Ignited the American Energy Revolution and Changed the World*. New York, NY: Simon & Schuster, 2014.

John Graves. *Fracking: America's Alternative Energy Revolution*, Ventura, CA: Safe Harbor, 2012.

Richard Heinberg. *Snake Oil: How Fracking's False Promise of Plenty Imperils Our Future*. Santa Rosa, CA: Post Carbon Institute, 2013.

William Kucewiez. *Fracking and Health: Fact vs. Fiction*. New York, NY: American Council on Science and Health, 2014.

Ezra Levant. *Groundswell: The Case For Fracking*. New York, NY: McClelland and Stewart, 2014.

Andrew Nikiforuk. *Slick Water: Fracking and One Insider's Stand Against the World's Most Powerful Industry*, Vancouver, Canada: Greystone Books, 2015

Gary Sernovitz. *The Green and the Black: The Complete Story of the Shale Revolution, the Fight Over Fracking, and the Future of Energy*. New York, NY: St. Martin's Press, 2016.

Michael Sylvester. *Environmental Science Report; Soils, Agricultural Water Pollution, Atmospheric Pollution, Fracking*. Amazon Digital Services, 2017.

Alan Tootill. *Fracking in the UK Volumes 1 and 2* (independently published), 2017.

Tom Wilber. *Under the Surface: Fracking, Fortunes, and the Fate of the Marcellus Shale*. Ithaca, NY: Cornell University Press, 2015.

Gregory Zuckerman. *The Frackers: The Outrageous Inside Story of the New Billionaire Wildcatters*, New York, NY: Penguin, 2013.

Periodicals and Internet Sources

BBC News, "What Is Fracking and Why Is it Controversial?" December 16, 2015. http://www.bbc.com/news/uk-14432401.

Mariah Blake, "How Hillary Clinton's State Department Sold Fracking to the World," Mother Jones, October 2014. http://www.motherjones.com/environment/2014/09/hillary-clinton-fracking-shale-state-department-chevron.

Susan L. Brantley and Anna Meyendorff, "The Facts on Fracking," The New York Times, March 13, 2013. http://www.nytimes.com/2013/03/14/opinion/global/the-facts-on-fracking.html.

Anna Kuchment, "Drilling for Earthquakes," Scientific American," March 28, 2016. https://www.scientificamerican.com/article/drilling-for-earthquakes/.

Patrick G. Lee, "EPA Concludes Fracking a Threat to U.S. Water Supplies," ProPublica, December 14, 2016. https://www.propublica.org/article/epa-concludes-fracking-a-threat-to-u.s.-water-supplies.

Seamus McGraw, "Is Fracking Safe? The 10 Most Controversial Claims About Natural Gas Drilling," Popular Mechanics, May 1, 2016. http://www.popularmechanics.com/science/energy/g161/top-10-myths-about-natural-gas-drilling-6386593/.

Vauhini Vara, "How Frackers Beat OPEC," The Atlantic, January/February 2017. https://www.theatlantic.com/magazine/archive/2017/01/how-frackers-beat-opec/508760.

Alexandra Zissu, "How to Tackle Fracking in Your Community," NRDC, January 27, 2016. https://www.nrdc.org/stories/how-tackle-fracking-your-community.

Index

F

G

H

I